God Bless
Deacon Peaces & Peggy Zaur

Have a great Forever!
Deacon Ray & Pat Duthoy

Thank you For allowing
Me To Serve
D. Ron Erbar

May our mighty Lord be with you always Hugs Teresa St. Boniface
Deacon Tom + Shelly McLuin

Gracias por todo = Thanks for all
Dcn. Freddy & Suly Hernan...

...cias por todo
& Martha

May God Bless you
Deacon Son & Rose

...op Brown,
my best wishes on a fruitful retirement.
God Bless and be with you.
Deacon Paul & Arlene Armonino

God Bless
Jimmy & ...py Espinoza

God's blessings to you.
John Erbar
Mavis P. Erhard

Good luck & God Bless
from a former Union Pacific employee!
Deacon Larry Mucho & Chris

Thank you for changing my life,
Deacon Joe Wallace
and ...

Dios la Bendiga siempre
God Bless you Always
Deacon Jose y Yolanda Campos

En este cambio de su vida esperamos que Dios los siga bendiciendo en ora buena
Rigo y Odelia Maldonado
2005

MAY "God" Bless You Always
Diacons Danny Bonn

May God Bless you
Deacon Carl & Candace Anderson

Be good!
Deacon Manuel Chavira

Wishing all the best & blessings
Deacon Bill & Jacquie Schlater

With Great Love, respect and admiration for all you did for God here in Orange!
Mary Chavez

Thank you for loving deacons and trusting Frank!

May God's Blessings Be with you always!
Deacon Gary & Christine Mucho

you have been & shall always be a great friend thank you. Gerry & Socorro De Santos

May God Blessed You our Hope with you all the way
Deacon Bill Young

Thank you Bishop [illegible] Brown [illegible] your [illegible] [illegible] service [illegible] [illegible] [illegible] [illegible] [illegible] Deacon [illegible] [illegible]

Thank you for all your Devoted leadership May God Bless you always

Deacon Ramirez & Elena Ramirez

Dear Bishop Brown:
Happy retirement and God Bless you!
Carlos & Elva Quiroga

With love in Christ our Savior
Deacon Louis Pluta St. Boniface church.

Dear Bishop Brown,
Thank you so much for your service to the faithful in the Diocese of Orange. May God reward you abundantly for it and for your continued ministry wherever you may be from here.
Blessings always.
Deacon Rey & Dee Marin

Dear Bishop Brown,
Thank you for your outstanding leadership as the Shepherd of the Diocese. Wishing you many blessings in your retirement. We will miss you.
In Christ,
Deacon Chuck & Yolande Dordy

Deacon Rafael & Delia Romero
1990

Dear Bishop Brown,
Thank you for your support giving to the Chinese Ministry. May God continuously bless you abundantly. Deacon Louis & Pearl Lin

Thanks for All Your Support Diaconate Community all these years
JB [illegible]

Bishop Tod
Thank you truly for the years of your life you gave to us as Bishop
we've been blessed and we will miss you. ~~and~~ hope ~~to~~ see you, enjoy your retirement sincerly Angela & Guillermo

Bishop Tod,
wishing you a long & enjoyable Retirment. Thank you for all you gave to Orange.
Deacon Don + Dottie Jensen

Santa Fe
—all the way
Volume 1: 1940s - 1966
By Bill Marvel

Published by
Morning Sun Books, Inc.
9 Pheasant Lane
Scotch Plains, NJ 07076

Library of Congress
Catalog Card No. 98-066807

First Printing
ISBN 1-58248-009-5

Color separation and printing by
The Kutztown Publishing Co., Inc.
Kutztown, Pennsylvania

Dedication
To Geoff, my son and computer guru

Acknowledgements

Even though the Santa Fe we knew no longer exists, it still has thousands of fans and modelers. As a consequence, few roads have been researched as thoroughly and meticulously. This book leans heavily upon the labors of a number of Santa Fe railfan-scholars. To mention just a few:

John McCall, author of four absolutely fundamental books on the railroad's motive power and practices—*Iron Horses of the Santa Fe Trail, Santa Fe Early Diesel Daze, The Doodlebugs,* and *Coach, Cabbage and Caboose*—graciously made time available to answer questions and solve a few Santa Fe riddles. Every railroad should have a John McCall.

Donald Duke, whose ongoing series, *Santa Fe: The Railroad Gateway to the American West,* chronicles an important part of the Santa Fe saga, helped to identify the location of a crucial picture, right down to the street intersection—and helpfully provided a map.

Journalist and author Fred W. Frailey's *A Quarter Century of Santa Fe Consists* is a work so basic and important to the understanding of Santa Fe's passenger business that one wonders why fans of other roads have not followed his example.

Karl Zimmerman's *Santa Fe Streamliners,* Jared W. Harper's *Raton Pass,* and Lloyd Stagner's *Santa Fe Steam Finale* and *Santa Fe 1940-1971 In Color* four volume set all demonstrate how much useful information can be packed into small books. The inestimable Mr. Stagner, who four times traveled this same track before me, seems able to pull any needed bit of information about the railroad out of his mind or his files at a moment's notice. In addition, the various motive power annuals by Joe McMillan, Robert C. Del Grosso, Bill Shippen, Joseph Shine and Kevin EuDaly were constantly at hand.

Anybody who wants to sample the astonishing flow of data on all things Santa Fe is directed to the Santa Fe Railway Historical & Modeling Society, its excellent publication, *The Warbonnet,* and its web site at www.ATSFRR.com/. Another useful cache of Santa Fe data can be found on the ATSF Internet Resource Center at www.playground.net/~atsf/.

Deep thanks to Lloyd Keyser, who interrupted his own Morning Sun project to offer sage advice and slides; to Bill Childers, for making his sharp eye and his memory for detail available; to Jay Miller, John Signor, Vernon Glover, and Wallace Abbey; and to the ever helpful Ed Seay. And a special thanks to Chard Walker, who always had a friendly greeting for railfans (including, one afternoon, this one) at Cajon Summit. As always, Bob Yanosey delivered a gentle but firm push at the right times and his intelligent guidance and faith in this project, kept everything on track.

Finally, my admiration to the photographers whose work made this book possible. Despite their best efforts to label slides and accurately recall locations and dates, and in spite of the excellent counsel and advice from the Santa Fe experts mentioned above, mistakes, like bad-order cars, will inevitably find their way into any consist. Railfans are often unforgiving of errors, especially if those errors concern their favorite railroad. I hope they will realize the responsibility has been mine and not that of the photographers who loaned their pictures or the experts who gave their advice.

Santa Fe Timeline

Santa Fe—all the way

In 1954, about the time many railfans were switching from black and white film to Kodachrome, Trains & Travel magazine, as Trains then called itself, devoted an entire issue to the Atchison Topeka & Santa Fe.

"Super Railroad," the magazine called it.

Anyone who had the opportunity to watch Santa Fe operate alongside the other big railroads of the West knew exactly what the magazine meant. Not bigger or longer or busier. But leaner, faster, somehow smarter. Even that then-formidable transportation machine, Union Pacific, did not do business with the flair of the Santa Fe.

Santa Fe's gross income had been third among all the railroads, at $80.3 million. But net income was $70.7 million, higher even than SP, UP or mighty Pennsy. The highest in the business, in fact. Operating ratio - the number of pennies the railroad spent to make a buck - was 70.03, compared to an industry average of 76.1. Santa Fe was able to pay cash for its new diesels and cars, and it had set up a fund to retire all outstanding bonds by 1995.

The road was conservative in its motive power practices and operations. Yet it was first with diesels, eliminating steam from whole divisions before other roads had even a single diesel freighter on the property. Smallest of the so-called "Super Seven" freight railroads, Santa Fe made up in hustle what it lacked in muscle. It ran proportionately more intermodal traffic than other roads. And really ran it. The Super C was the fastest freight train in the world.

But Santa Fe had something else not easily translated to the bottom line. It had style.

No other railroad cultivated a regional identification as assiduously as Santa Fe. When its rails reached California in 1897, Santa Fe was the only transcontinental whose tracks stretched in an unbroken line all the way back to Chicago. Thus a slogan was born: "SANTA FE-all the way."

This was more than an advertising blurb to paint on the side of boxcars. Railroad historians and economists write of the "Natural Territory" of a railroad. The Natural Territory of the Santa Fe was that vast region roughly south and west of Kansas City, the American Southwest, where for almost a century the road was virtually unchallenged.

Santa Fe didn't just serve the Southwest. It was the Southwest, from the famous Warbonnet emblazoned on its diesels to the Southwest decor in its dining cars to the Southwest and Mission Revival architecture of its stations (an idea of Edward P. Ripley, who was one of the road's greatest presidents). Chico, the Navajo boy, graced its public timetables and its magazine and newspaper ads until the end of passenger service. Navajo Indians worked the railroad's track gangs. They boarded the road's great passenger trains in Gallup and rode through to Albuquerque, pointing out lineside points of interest to passengers. When those passengers detrained at Albuquerque to stretch their legs, they found Indians on the platform selling native arts and crafts. And, in 1974, the first American Indian promoted to the right-hand side of a locomotive cab was Louis R. Abeyta, a member of the Laguna Pueblo and an employee of Santa Fe's Coast Division.

When the road created its new streamliner SUPER CHIEF in 1936, advertising manager Roger Birdseye, an authority on Indian tribes of the Southwest, named the cars after Indian pueblos in New Mexico and Arizona. Birdseye was following the long Santa Fe tradition of enlightened managers who understood that the railroad was selling not just its services but a geographic region. In 1895, traffic manager W.F. White bought the rights to Thomas Moran's monumental painting of the Grand Canyon (page 77), and, in an inspired public relations campaign, dispatched thousands of reproductions to on-line schools, banks, hotels, and whoever else would display them. Five years later, William Haskell Simpson, the road's new general advertising agent, began sending artists to the Grand Canyon and other locations along the line to paint landscapes that would be used on the railroad's posters and calendars and in its magazine advertisements. For years, Santa Fe offered free passage to any artist who agreed to paint Southwest scenes and give one painting to the railroad. One of those artists, E. Irving Couse, painted the portrait of an Indian chief that, in a highly stylized version, graced the flanks of Santa Fe's first passenger diesels. The museum-quality collection of the Southwestern art Santa Fe gathered through the 1930s still could be seen hanging on the office walls in the company's Schaumburg, Illinois, headquarters as late as 1995.

But SANTA FE-all the way meant more than Indians and mesas and cactus. It also evoked the high-rise towers of Chicago, the rolling wheat fields of Kansas, the nodding oil wells of Oklahoma and Texas, the glamor of Southern California. And, all but unnoticed, the piney woods of southeast Texas and neighboring Louisiana.

For those of us who gathered along the track over the years, all this was an inseparable part of the road's appeal. There was something special about photographing trains on a blistering July afternoon at, say, Newton, Kansas, then stepping into the Harvey House restaurant for a bowl of homemade vanilla ice cream. You knew that you were tasting a half-century of Santa Fe tradition.

(Right) *Along the Santa Fe Trail: Somewhere in Western Kansas, RSD5 2128 trundles westward with a work train in June, 1965. This is the heart of the historic Santa Fe, the original 1872 route that followed the old Santa Fe Trail—as the sign reminds us—from Newton west to Raton Pass and then south to Lamy, New Mexico. Generations of merchants, trappers, traders and settlers passed this way after 1821, and Cyrus K. Holliday, father of the Santa Fe, predicted that a railroad that followed their path would make money. And so it has. But this line, 100-mph territory, is the route of most of the road's passenger fleet. And it is freight that now pays the bills. (Emery J. Gulash)*

The idea of this book, then, is to step out of the harsh glare of the present for a spell. To soak up the Santa Fe tradition. Our first volume will cover from the 1940s to 1966, the fateful year that Santa Fe took the first steps towards eliminating its first-class passenger trains, when it became a little less the Santa Fe we had known. The second volume will pick up the story and continue to the end, and absorption into that strange hybrid beast, Burlington Northern Santa Fe.

It says a great deal about the power of Santa Fe's image over the years that in 1995 management of the combined railroad announced that, for the time being, at least, new diesels would continue to be delivered in the famous Warbonnet scheme. One might well have asked, just who was absorbing whom?

Come ride these rails,
mainline and obscure branch alike, as we travel
Santa Fe—all the way

—Bill Marvel, 1998

▲▲▲▲▲▲▲▲▲▲▲▲▲▲▲▲▲▲

(Below) *Santa Fe shares its rails with rival Union Pacific over Cajon. But on Sept. 7, 1966, it is blue and yellow SD24s that swing into the cut west of the 3823-foot Summit and begin the 3 percent descent to the Los Angeles Basin. The west leg of Summit wye, at right, has felt the weight of thousands of helpers over the years. Summit station and the house where relief operator and resident railfan Chard Walker has raised his family are sheltered under the large trees in the background. The layout here will soon change considerably. In the distance, arch-rival Southern Pacific is already at work on its Palmdale Cutoff over the pass, which will open next year. And in 1972, Santa Fe itself will realign three miles of track through here, straightening curves and lowering the elevation by 50 feet.* (Bill Marvel)

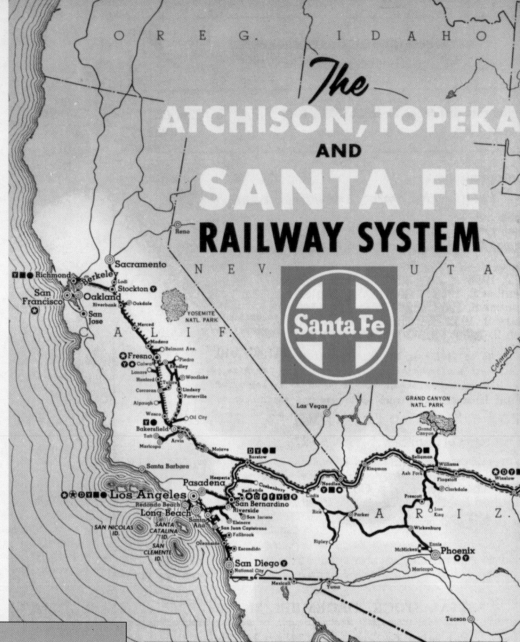

The **ATCHISON, TOPEKA** AND **SANTA FE** RAILWAY SYSTEM

Santa Fe

EXPLANATION

THE SYMBOLS BELOW REPRESENT MAJOR FACILITIES OF THE SANTA FE RAILWAY SYSTEM, AND ARE INDICATED ON THE MAP NEAR THE NAME OF THE TOWN IN WHICH THEY ARE LOCATED.

★ System Headquarters
✪ Grand Division Headquarters
✿ Division Headquarters
Ⓖ Diesel General Repair Shop
Ⓗ Diesel Heavy Maintenance Shop
Ⓜ Diesel Maintenance & Inspection
Ⓟ Passenger Car Shop
Ⓕ Freight Car Shop

▼ Major Freight Classification Yard
▽ Other Freight Yards
■ Principal Diesel Fueling Station
Ⓖ General Store
Ⓢ District Store
● Division Store
Ⓞ Local Store
Ⓡ Reclamation Point

Ⓦ Centralized Work Equipment Shop

▬▬▬ Single Track
▭▭▭ Multiple Track
◄▪▪► Trackage Rights
▬▬▬ Other Railroads
▬▬▬ Automatic Block Signals
▬▬▬ Traffic Control
▬▬▬ Automatic Train Control with Traffic Control
▬▬▬ Automatic Block Signals with Automatic Train Stop
▬▬▬ Traffic Control with Automatic Train Stop

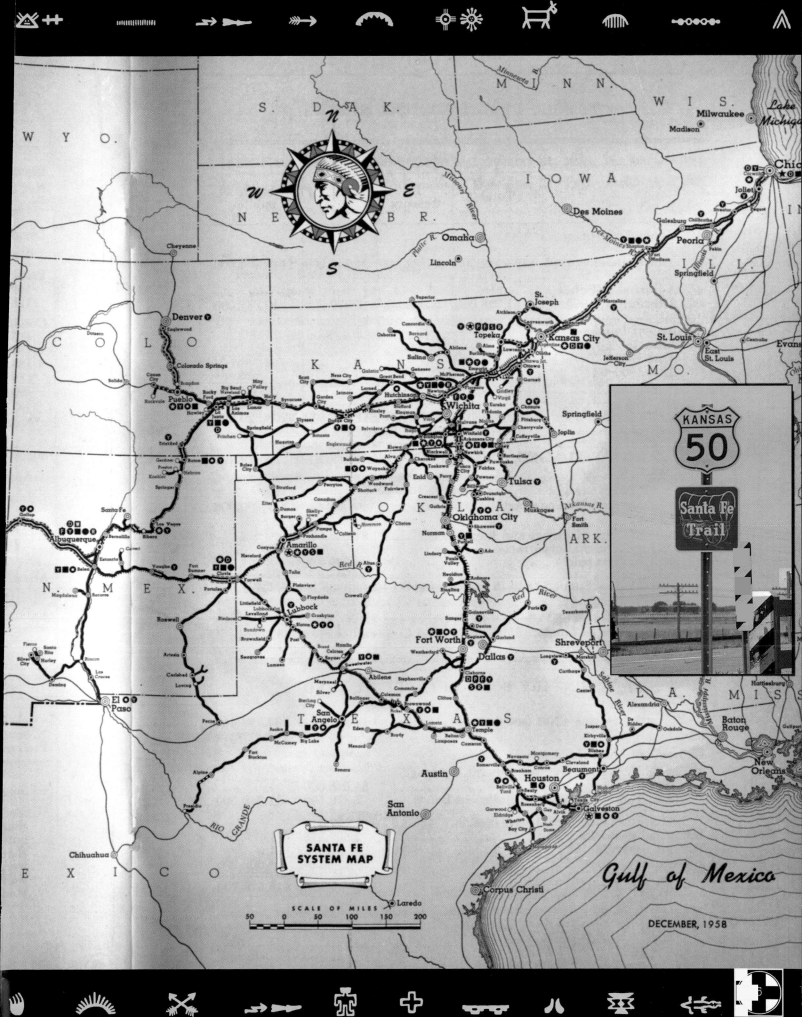

Santa Fe Timeline

THE 1940s

+ December, 1940: Santa Fe receives the first of its FTs, begins dieselization of freight operations west of Winslow, Ariz.
+ Last steam locomotives are delivered—2900-2929 series 4-8-4s in 1943/44, and 5011-5035 series 2-10-4s in 1944.
+ Alco 51LAB, the first PAs, purchased and put into service.
+ THE SUPER CHIEF and EL CAPITAN begin daily operation in February, 1948.
+ April, 1948: Chicago-Galveston TEXAS CHIEF innaugurated.
+ Total revenue, 1949: $487.7 million. Net income: $50 million

Loaded for War

Take a good look at this picture. It shows a Santa Fe train loaded for war.

That war train is ready to roll. It is going through!

In railroad language, it has the right-of-way over everything else on the line.

So it must be with all American transportation until this war job is done.

Victory Rides on Wheels

This is essentially a war of rolling wheels.

Millions of men and tens of millions of tons of vital foods, raw materials, and finished products must be moved swiftly and surely, where and when they are needed.

Stop the wheels that move them, and we stop all that floats and flies as well.

That is why, on the Santa Fe, movements essential to the war effort are topping the greatest transportation job in all our history. They must come first, beyond argument or selfish interest.

★ During 1942, with 70% fewer locomotives, Santa Fe moved 123% more freight ton-miles and 79% more military and civilian passenger-miles than in 1918, during the First World War. The Army and Navy, the ODT, and civilian shippers and travelers everywhere are cooperating 100% with the railroads of America in making records like this possible.

SERVING THE SOUTHWEST FOR 70 YEARS

Santa Fe

(Left) In the late 1940s, 4-6-2s such as the 3443, shown backing down to Los Angeles Union Passenger Terminal with one of the San Bernardino locals, still dominate local passenger service out of Los Angeles, and three of the heavy Pacifics are assigned to Los Angeles and two to the Valley. The 3443 remains a prime example of the quiet revolution wrought by Santa Fe's longtime chief of motive power John Purcell in the years just after World War I, when he created a series of designs that were steady, sturdy, with nothing fancy. Unlike 45 of her 50 sister engines, the 3443 escaped the railroad's 1937-1947 modernization campaign, and it will go for scrap in February, 1952, still looking pretty much the way it did when it rolled off Baldwin's erecting floor in 1924. *(Steve Bogen)*

(Above) Train 42, the morning Los Angeles-San Bernardino local, threads the six-track approach to Los Angeles Union Passenger Terminal on its way to the Pasadena Subdivision for a leisurely two and a half hour run. At Mission Tower, which is just behind the photographer, the three-car train, dubbed the "Chippewa Chief" by local railfans, will turn north and follow the west bank of the Los Angeles River, cross the river at Main Street and begin the climb along the San Gabriel foothills. In 1950, the 56-mile Second District sees 11 passenger trains a day, and despite steep grades and numerous speed restrictions, it will remain the road's principal passenger route out of LA, surviving to become part of Metrolink.

(Below) Sometimes the rarity of an otherwise poorly lit and out of focus slide overcomes our tendency to discard it as is the case with this vintage scene. Medium Mikado 3140, another John Purcell design, trundles the Second Subdivision local freight along Pasadena Avenue near Figueroa in the late 1940s. The weekday run will continue to Azusa, where it will exchange cars with its westbound counterpart out of San Bernardino, most likely behind another 3100. Built in 1916, engines 3129-3158 almost all ended up assigned to Los Angeles, where they found employment on Second District local freights, on the San Diego line, and even occasional helper service on Cajon. *(both, Don Ball Collection)*

(Above) We are looking down on Winslow, Arizona,
sometime in the late-1940s. Headquarters of the 688-
mile-plus Albuquerque Division, Winslow is probably
the only town on the Santa Fe named for the president of
another railroad-Edward Winslow, financier and president in the 1880s of the Saint Louis-San Francisco. It
was Frisco-owned Atlantic & Pacific Railroad that built
the line through here in 1882. By 1890 when Santa Fe
acquired Frisco, and A&P, Winslow was already a thriving settlement.

Refrigerator cars fill the tracks near the bottom of the
picture, because Winslow is the location of a large plant
that replenishes the ice on fruit and vegetable shipments
from Arizona and California. Beyond is the 35-stall
roundhouse with its 120-foot turntable, long enough to
accommodate a 2-10-4 should one find its way this far
west.

Winslow was once the place where westbound trains
exchanged coal-burning for oil-burning engines. But
during World War II, when trains were arriving or departing the 33-track yard every 12 minutes on average, Santa
Fe dieselized freight operations west to Barstow almost
at a stroke with 68 FTs. The roundhouse is divided into
a 27-stall steam section and a 14-stall addition for
diesels, separated by an asbestos fire wall. But there's
nary a diesel to be seen today.

A glance at the track profiles reveal another reason for
the large roundhouse: Winslow, elevation 4856 feet, sits
at the bottom of a sag between two stiff grades, the 0.6%
climb 128 miles east to Gallup, and the 96-mile 1.42%
grade west to the Arizona Divide and Supai, the second
longest helper district on anybody's railroad. Steam or
diesel, this is one busy place. *(Don Ball Collection)*

(Left) In August 1941 the photographer and a group of friends have taken the day off from an NMRA convention in Peoria to do a little railfanning. Following a Rock Island freight north, they stopped off to take a few in pictures in Chillicothe and at Houlihan's Curve and now they are 6 miles west, at the top of the hill at Edelstein just in time to catch this Santa Fe freight slogging westbound behind a heavy Mike. The 3160-4000 series 2-8-2s are standard freight power from Chicago to Shopton, Iowa, but freights usually require another 2-8-2 pushing up 1.1% Edelstein Hill. The helper will cut off about a mile east of the station, cross over and back down the hill.

(Emery J. Gulash)

(Below) Chillicothe in the early 1950s is headquarters of the Illinois Division, the first division point west of Chicago. Here, midmorning, train 11, THE KANSAS CITYAN behind E6s 15 and 15A, pauses for a crew change before resuming its 451-mile, 445-minute dash for Kansas City. It will arrive at 4:55 p.m., plenty of time for passengers to freshen up and head for a restaurant for one of those good Kansas City steaks. The 2,000-hp units were built in 1941 for service on THE SUPER CHIEF and EL CAPITAN, and will roll right into the late 1960s on Tulsa and Dallas trains. *(Don Ball Collection)*

(Above) Train 18, THE SUPER CHIEF, has arrived at Dearborn Station at 1:45 p.m., Sept. 22, 1949, and, passengers unloaded, is now being backed down to the 18th Street coach yard. Reequipped just the year before and now running every other day, the streamliner is the pride of Santa Fe's transcontinental fleet, advertised in the pages of *Life, Collier's, The National Geographic* and *The Saturday Evening Post*. F3 21, delivered in December, 1946, has already been modified by Santa Fe, which has removed the middle porthole, installed a rotating Mars light in the nose and moved the headlight to the middle of the door.

(William Echternach, NRHS Collection)

(Below) Elsewhere in Chicago this pleasant September afternoon, down on the Lakefront, visitors to the 1948-49 Chicago Railroad Fair are exploring a brand 6,000-hp set of F7s, right off the erecting floor at EMD. This is the first of 462 F7s the road will eventually roster. Also on the fair grounds, visitors can see a Milwaukee Bi-polar, a GG-1, New York Central's Poppet-valve 4-8-4 #5500, a Union Pacific Big Boy and Burlington's Zephyr. But it is Santa Fe 202 that points the way to the future. (Steve Bogen)

(Above) Proudly wearing the Warbonnet passenger scheme, FT set 162L-A-B-C have come over the pass from Trinidad unassisted with #17, THE SUPER CHIEF on March 26, 1949. The train has paused for servicing and inspection at Raton, the fireman is climbing the steps to the cab, and departure is just minutes away. Meanwhile, alongside the first booster unit, a couple of repairmen are working furiously on what appears to be a sticking brake cylinder. Delivered as freighters, the 4-unit FTs have been rebuilt for passenger service, regeared along with 36 sister-units for 95 mph and equipped with gyrating Mars lights. The boosters have new boilers and enlarged water tanks. All will be returned to freight service by 1951 as new passenger F3s arrive to relieve them from duty.

(Below) Brake problems attended to, 17 resumes its westward journey. With re-equipment, the train's Chicago-Los Angeles schedule has been speeded up to the prewar standard, 39 hours, 45 minutes, and within a few miles the units will soon be hitting the authorized 79 miles an hour.

(Both, Ross Grenard collection)

Santa Fe Timeline

1950

+ Santa Fe acquires the first of 250 GP7s
+ April 2: THE KANSAS CITY CHIEF added to the schedule
+ Total revenue: $534.6 million. Net income: $82.1 million

POTASH
Plenty in American Mines and Brines

The earliest colonists on the Atlantic seaboard set up tiny plants for leaching wood ashes. They boiled down the lye in iron kettles. The residue was a white solid, used in making soap. They called this residue "potash," because it was made in pots, from ashes. Today potash comes into our daily lives in a hundred ways. The term is now applied to cover most of the compounds of potassium—a soft, light, silver-white metal of the alkali metal group. Immense quantities of potassium compounds, or potash, are used in the preparation of fertilizers. Potash, too, enters into the varied products of a score of industries, from soap and starches and medicines, to glass ● Commercial production of potash in America from wood ashes declined with the clearing of the land. Before our Civil War, potash salts had been found in German mines and brine wells, and that country became chief source of a chemical vital to modern agriculture and industry ● The World War brought us a "potash famine," stimulated intensive search for adequate domestic supplies. Discovery and development of enormous potash deposits in the earth near Carlsbad, New Mexico, followed, supplemented by increasing production from the desert brine of Searles Lake.

● Over 90% of all American potash comes from the great mines near Carlsbad, New Mexico. Carry two produced there—thousands of carloads annually—reveals how ads-vances are borne by rails ● Long privileged to come in seeking its transportation problems, the Santa Fe pays high tribute to the tonnage and virtue of all those, including the American Potash Institute, who have helped to develop this vital American industry.

(Above) Normally assigned to freight service between La Junta and Albuquerque, the 3804 finds itself northbound out of Belen on the El Paso-Albuquerque line. The 31-year-old Baldwin appears to have been freshly outshopped at Albuquerque and perhaps is returning from a shakedown run. Although dieselization is within sight, a number of the 2-10-2s have received new speed recorders, Type E radial buffers between the 20,000-gallon tender and engine, and Security circulators in the firebox. The 3804 will last almost to the end of steam, going to scrap in 1955.

(Below) Fireman and head brakeman give the photographer the once-over as the big 2-10-2 plods on. Notwithstanding the road's fine Northerns and its superlative Texas types, the 2-10-2s were Santa Fe's biggest single motive-power success until the coming of the diesel. An outgrowth of experiments with a couple 2-10-0s, the 2-10-2 wheel arrangement was to carry the Santa Fe name far and wide. And, they could haul. In the oil-burning version, the 3800s delivered a frame-busting 81,600 pounds tractive effort (coal burners 81,500 pounds). *(Both, Marvin H. Cohen)*

(Above) An engine with a very un-Santa Fe look, 2-8-0 2519 leads freight units through the yard at Vaughn, New Mexico, in 1950. A little west of its usual haunts down on the Slayton Division in Texas and on Kansas branch-line locals, the 1907 Brooks-built engine has been shopped at Albuquerque and is working its way back home. It is one of 47 2-8-0s acquired in 1929 when Santa Fe took over the Kansas City, Mexico & Orient, most ex-New York Central engines. All are popular with crews and ideal branch-line power.

(Below) A New Mexico spring thunderstorm is brewing in the south as one of John Purcell's classic 2-8-2s, 3222, plods along somewhere near Isletta with an engine DIT-dead in tow-for the Albuquerque shops. From the scrap boiler-tube pilot to the Elesco feedwater heater below the smokebox, the centered unvisored headlight, illuminated number board behind the stack, and closely-grouped sand domes, the heavy Mike has that Santa Fe "look." In spring,1950, the Albuquerque-El Paso line remains 100 percent steam, while elsewhere on the system, the storage tracks are full of dead steamers. But bumper crops of potatoes, melons, onions and winter wheat, and, on June 25, the North Korean invasion of South Korea, will soon put Santa Fe steam power back to work.

(Both, Marvin H. Cohen)

(Left) Between Argentine Yards and Kansas City Union Station, Santa Fe's tracks follow the Kansas River bottoms, where E3A 13 is just coming east with #12, THE CHICAGOAN. The seven E3s-four cab units and three boosters-were Electro-Motive Corporation's first true production units, that is, the first diesel locomotives EMC manufactured itself rather than assembled from components. In Kansas City, train 12 will be combined with train 212, THE TULSAN, for a 2 p.m. departure for Chicago.

(Below) Midway between Emporia and Topeka, #12 rockets past the station at Burlingame, Kansas. THE CHICAGOAN knocks off the 200 miles from Newton to Kansas City in 198 minutes, much of it on the Eastern Division's First District, the original line via Topeka. THE KANSAS CITYAN, THE TULSAN and CALIFORNIA LIMITED follow this line. The California streamline fleet, on the other hand, follows the Ottawa cutoff to Kansas City. The Burlingame station is fondly remembered by railfans. In later years, station agent Bud Goebel kept a small museum of Santa Fe memorabilia on display there in honor of his late son, Kenny.

(Both, Don Ball Collection)

(Right) The sun was barely up this September day, 1950, when M.157 set out with train #15 from Fort Madison, Iowa, for the 224-mile, 6-hour 17-minute run over the main line to Kansas City, one of the the most demanding motorcar runs on the Santa Fe. Now, a little after 2 p.m., the car has left its trailer in the station and idles at Kansas City Terminal Tower 5, awaiting movement to Argentine Yard for servicing and inspection. At 6:30 p.m., she'll depart eastward as train #16, pulling into Fort Madison at 1:10 a.m., just an hour ahead of #4, the CALIFORNIA LIMITED. (J.J.Buckley)

Santa Fe Timeline

1951

+ July: Kansas River floods, halting Kansas City rail operations for several weeks
+ Santa Fe opens a hump-retarder yard in Pueblo, Colo., its second after Argentine
+ CTC installed over Raton Pass
+ THE SUPER CHIEF re-equipped with with new dining and lounge cars and Pleasure Domes
+ Total revenue: $582.7 million. Net income: $73.3 million

(Above) Engineer and fireman have lowered the sun visors as FT 185 swings past Kansas City Union Station and into the afternoon sun with an westbound extra, Aug. 11, 1951. Over the years, Santa Fe played subtle variations on its basic dark blue and yellow freight paint scheme. This all-blue "experimental" scheme started appearing around January on about a dozen of the freighters. The experiment will not judged a success, however, and by 1952, the road will be repainting them in the standard scheme. One of the last FTs delivered to the road, in August 1945, the lead unit here originally wore number 179L. But when Santa Fe rearranged many of the A-B-B-A FTs into A-B-B configuration, the new sets were renumbered into the 180LAB-199LAB series, with the extra cab units retaining their original number. Some of the FTs will be renumbered six times before being traded in on GP20s and 30s. *(Don Ball Collection)*

(Right) It's no holiday for the baggageman-brakeman who already has the door open as M.183 rolls into McCook, Ill., at 2 p.m. on the Fourth of July, 1951. This is the first stop out of Chicago for train #13 to Pekin, a run the EMC-Pullman motorcar has held since 1945, when it took the place of the wrecked M.185. Notoriously nose-heavy and roughriding, especially when running without a trailer, the 80-foot RPO-baggage-smoker-coach seats 20 passengers in coach and 11 in the smoking section. It will finish its long career out west, working the Wichita, Kan.-San Angelo, Tex., run.

Telescoping stack scissored up, Northern 3775 smokes past Turner with westbound empty reefers, August 11, 1951. The engine is assigned to Argentine-Waynoka through freights, the last big stand for the 4-8-4s. Baldwin-built in 1938, the 3775 should be good for years of service: 10 months ago it received a new carbon steel boiler, replacing the original nickel steel boiler, which was subject to stress cracking along the seams. Though officially rated at 66,000 pounds tractive effort, these engines have delivered as much as 75,200 pounds on dynamometer tests. With 300 pounds boiler pressure, they're easily capable of running 100 mph.
(Don Ball Collection)

(Below) The engineer watches as workers unload express from the the baggage compartment of M.186, the car assigned to the Pekin run on July 22. The motorcar runs are labor-intensive, requiring an engineer, conductor, mail clerk, and baggage handle-brakeman. Like the M.183, this car ran for years with a distillate-burning 400-hp EMC engine, but because of rising gasoline prices it was dieselized a year ago when the Wichita shops installed a new Caterpillar D-397. At the end of the year, Santa Fe's 39 active motorcars will still command 18 runs, racking up more than 2 million passenger miles.

(Left) The 153-mile Pekin run calls for M.186 to arrive in Streator at 4 p.m. and pull into Pekin at 6 p.m., hardly a strain on the car, which is equipped with ATS and a speed recorder and capable of batting along at 65 mph. Three motorcars usually rotate on the schedule, allowing each to run every third day on train #25-26 from Streator to Shopton, Iowa, for maintenance. The M.186 will last until one cold winter's night in November, 1963, when a careless employee neglects to connect the car's water heater to the engine's cooling system during a layover in Kiowa, Kansas, resulting in a cracked engine block. *(All, J.J.Buckley)*

(Above) Two days later finds M.184, the relief car on the Chicago-Pekin schedule, pulling into Joliet Union Station at 2:40 p.m. This has been M.184's home territory since 1931, when the car was one of two ordered by Santa Fe for the Chicago-Pekin and Streator-Shopton runs. The other car, M.185, was destroyed in a fiery crash in 1945 when it was broad-sided by a B&O 4-8-2, rupturing the fuel tank and igniting 520 gallons of distillate.

(Below) M.184 resumes its journey. Number 13 will run west to Ancona, near Streator, then depart the main line and putter down the 55-mile branch to Pekin.

From 1928 to 1931 in the depths of the Great Depression, Santa Fe set out to lower expenses on marginal passenger runs by ordering 43 motor-cars, most, like the M.184, EMC-Pullman model 148s, named for the EMC 148 gasoline engine. Motorcar operations peaked in 1934, when 43 cars held down 39 schedules, including several overnight runs with Pullman sleeping cars. (Both, J.J. Buckley)

Santa Fe Timeline

1952

✚ RDC-1 service innaugurated Los Angeles-San Diego
✚ Total revenue: $616.8 million. Net income: $70.7 million

(*Above*) Drivers churning, heavy 4-6-2 3441 heads out of Kansas City Union Station on a frosty January morning in 1952, probably with Second #7, MAIL AND EXPRESS. The Pacific will see the train as far as Newton. Constructed in 1924 by Baldwin, Santa Fe's favorite builder, and rebuilt at Topeka in 1944, this is a thoroughly modern Pacific and a testimony to the soundness of John Purcell's original design.

(*Left*) Two days after Christmas, 1952, with the holiday rush behind them, E6A 13 and F7A 45 share the Argentine ready tracks with a 2900-series 4-8-4. The E6 will probably go out on THE TULSAN this afternoon and the F7 is assigned to one of the California streamliners. The Northern most likely is destined for a freight run west.

(Both, Don Ball Collection)

(Above) Despite the presence of a few diesels, Argentine in April, 1952, is still the smoky stronghold of Santa Fe's remaining steam engines, which dominate freight service west to Clovis, N.M. The roundhouse is at right. A newly-delivered RSD5 idles in the middle distance. The 3462, one of the road's magnificent Hudsons; a Baldwin switcher; Northerns and FT sets gather around the distant coaling tower. Meanwhile, plans are already being drawn for the new diesel shop on this site.

(Below) The brakeman rides the pilot as 4-8-4 3779 moves off down the yard to take on a westbound freight. In the 1952 annual report, Santa Fe President F.G. Gurley will promise that by the end of 1953, Santa Fe will retain only "the best of steam engines" for service, guaranteeing the 3779 and its 64 sisters at least another year of employment. Long after many other roads have shut down their steam shops, in fact, Santa Fe Northerns and 2-10-4 Texas types are still receiving class repairs at Albuquerque. (Both, Don Ball Collection)

(Above) The 3772 rolls westbound reefers past Holliday Tower, 6.3 miles west of Turner, Feb. 10, 1952. Just ahead lies the .6% climb up Olathe Hill. Having lingered at Argentine, she'll have to top off that big 20,000-gallon tank at Ottawa, about 55 miles west. Water will be taken again in another 100 miles at Aikman or 120 miles at Augusta. In about three hours, she'll pull into Wellington, where another 4-8-4 will be waiting to take her place. Oiled, watered, and sand supply replenished, the 3772 will be held to relay the next westbound. (Don Ball Collection)

(Below) Several hundred miles from home rails, 3930 takes a sip from a Union Pacific water plug at Fremont, Neb., on Oct. 27, 1952. The biggest fall traffic rush since World War II has swamped UP, which has turned to its neighbors for additional motive power. Six 2-8-2s from Milwaukee Road and Illinois Central worked the east end, and five 2-10-2s and two 2-8-4s from Santa Fe have been working North Platte-Denver freights. But now their work is done, and the 3930 is headed home. One wonders what UP enginemen thought of the engine. When UP ordered its own 144 2-10-2s, Omaha listed them on the roster simply as TTTs, refusing to acknowledge the road that, after all, invented the wheel arrangement and gave it its name. By any name, the 3930 clearly can outpull UP's equivalent, delivering 85,600 pounds tractive effort to the TTT's 70,450. (Ray Lowry, Lou Schmitz Collection)

23

Santa Fe Timeline

1953

+ Business decline follows signing of truce in Korean War
+ 222 new diesels acquired; diesels now handle 96.5% of freight and 99.8% of passenger car miles
+ Total revenue: $626 million. Net income: $77.2 million

(Above) As it has done every day except Sunday since 1927, mixed train #67 rattles through Cunningham, Kan., on the 79.4-mile branch from Wichita out to Pratt. Formally known as the Wichita District, Panhandle Division, the line was begun in 1884 as the Wichita & Western and acquired by Santa Fe in 1898. This fine June morning, the usual GP7 has been called elsewhere, and Prairie 1004 is in charge of the miscellany of boxcars and the combine that will trundle out to Pratt, then return a couple hours later as #68. One of only fourteen 2-6-2s left on Santa Fe's roster, the engine emerged from Baldwin in 1901 as a 4-cylinder Vauclain compound, was simpled in 1923 at Topeka, and will go to scrap in just one year. Meantime, 67/68 will roll on until 1961, behind GP7s. *(Sanford Goodrick)*

(Below) With full dieselization only two years away, Santa Fe nevertheless will spend $4.7 million to shop steam locomotives in 1953, the last year they will receive class overhauls. Steam is going out in style, not on a few bedraggled plug runs but on hot perishable trains and manifests, more than 100 during the first half of July alone. All but one of the Northerns remain active-the 3785 remains in the Albuquerque shops awaiting a new boiler that will never be installed. The 3769, on the other hand, still runs with its original nickel-steel boiler and has cheated the scrap line so far.

(Above) Santa Fe was the first railroad to buy FTs, back on Oct. 1, 1940. It bought more of them than anyone else, and, on June 28, 1953, it still has the largest fleet. Some 319 of the original 320 units, including the 412A waiting for clearance on a westbound out of Argentine, still roam the rails. Delivered as the 147C in January, 1945, the last year Santa Fe purchased FTs, the 412 was renumbered and equipped with footboards for local freight service. But with the arrival of GP7s, it's been reassigned to through Houston-Argentine service.

(Below) If you wanted a picture of the good, the bad and the ugly on the Santa Fe, the place to be July 12, 1953 is AY Tower, where FT 190, an example of the most conspicuous success story in post-war railroading, and Alco DL-109 50LA, an equally conspicuous failure, momentarily and by chance occupy adjacent tracks. The 1,350-hp freighters, lineal descendants of the triumphant 1940 demonstrators, have made their reputation in both freight and passenger service, whereas 50LA, after only a single test run over Raton Pass, was banished forever to Santa Fe's flatlands, where it can run to its heart's content, at least until it's scrapped in a few years.

The 1953 summer perishable rush is underway by July 5. Santa Fe has 274 active steamers, including 63 of its 65 Northerns, which are moving 10 trains a day between Waynoka and Argentine. The road paid Baldwin $252,335.71 each in wartime dollars for the 2918 and her 29 sisters. For its money it got the heaviest and possibly the best 4-8-4s ever built, 510,150 pounds of engine delivering 4,950 hp at the drawbar. Moreover, the extra weight made the 2900s a better freight engine than the 499,600-pound 3776 class 4-8-4s, which could be slippery in freight service. *(Don Ball Collection)*

The 2904 is drifting down the .6% Mill Creek Valley grade at Zarah, milepost 16.2 out of Kansas City. The foot of the grade at Holliday is just three miles ahead. Within a month a bountiful summer harvest will be underway, filling the rails with "high yellow" reefer blocks from Arizona, California and Texas, and recalling steam from the storage lines at Argentine. *(Don Ball Collection)*

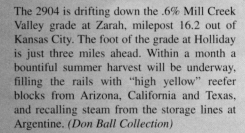

(Above) The head brakeman rides the pilot, ready to hop off and throw the switch at Turner, giving 3768 the open road. She'll make time: Every turn of those 80-inch drivers carries the 3768 another 22 feet 6 inches down the track. The 1938 Baldwin received a new carbon steel boiler in Dec., 1951. In 1958, the railroad will donate her to Wichita, Kan., where she'll go on display at Friends University. *(Don Ball Collection)*

26

(Above) The crews of the 3776 and the 2906 can sit back and relax now. They've brought their train in from Wellington or Waynoka and in a few minutes they'll tie up at Argentine, wash up, change and go home. The photographer is standing on the "high line" between Turner and Holliday, constructed after the catastrophic 1951 flood to give Santa Fe a dry route into Kansas City. The unusual doubleheader must be a power transfer. It's hard to imagine an eastbound that might require the combined 12,000-ton rating of these two engines. *(Don Ball Collection)*

(Above) On May 2, 1953 the Argentine roundhouse is full of passenger power. Pacific 3424, light Hudson 3455, the famous "Blue Goose" 3460 and sister 3462 are in the house, and 0-6-0T 9147, the regular Argentine shop goat, steams just outside. The Pacific will likely go out on a Tulsa train. The 3460 and 3455 are assigned to Kansas City-Newton service and the 3462 protects for the Kansas City-Chicago schedule. The 9147 will stay right here, never wandering more than a few hundred yards from the turntable until April, 1954, when it will be loaded on a flat car and shipped to Cleburne, Tex., to replace 9088, the shop switcher there. For brief periods over the next two years, the little tanker will be the only Santa Fe engine in steam. By next month, dieselization of THE OIL FLYER and THE ANTELOPE will send all six of the 3460-series 4-6-4s to the dead line, though they will be briefly resuscitated later in the year to power a series of Boy Scout specials.

(Above) A stepladder, an oil can, a wheelbarrow full of coiled hose and spare parts—the tools of the trade at a busy steam terminal litter the ground around the 3460. This was the Santa Fe's only streamlined steamer, though plans were made to streamline Northern 3765 until somebody calculated how much weight that would add to an already hefty locomotive. As it is, all the extra metal does not seem to hold back the 3460, which, with its 84-inch drivers and 300 pounds boiler pressure, is perfectly capable of breaking the century mark. Though slippery, the Hudson actually outperforms the Northerns at speeds over 50 mph. So, just how fast are Santa Fe's 3460s? "We'll never know," an engineer was once heard to say. "Nobody will have the guts to open them up all the way." (Both, Don Ball Collection)

(Above) Like a lady in a ball gown in a room full of workers in coveralls, the gleaming 3460 lends an air of elegance to the roundhouse leads at Argentine on July 11 in another faded photograph. A hostler climbs down from the cab. No longer in regular service, the engine is being groomed for a Boy Scout special, one of 20 Santa Fe will run west from Kansas City by July 14. *(Harold Henri, Lou Schmitz Collection)*

(Below) 3460's 20,000-gallon tender sparkles in the sunshine. But on Nov. 8, the engine has been relegated to the Argentine dead line, along with five of the other heavy 4-6-4s. Painted in two shades of blue, with blue-gray running gear, chromium-plated grab irons and brake wheels, and road number etched into the stainless steel strip and painted in chip-proof black enamel, the 3460 is all dressed up with nowhere to go. But in February, 1964, it will be pulled out of storage and buffed up to star in a company movie—about dieselization. *(Both, Don Ball Collection)*

(Above) Late afternoon sun lights up the stainless steel flanks of 21LABC, passenger F3s waiting Sept. 7, 1953, for 7 p.m. departure on THE SUPER CHIEF. Alongside THE ERIE LIMITED waits back under the train shed for a 6:05 p.m. departure while RS1s of both Santa Fe and Chicago & Western Indiana switch nearby tracks. Reequipped just two years before with new sleeping cars from Budd and American Car & Foundry, THE SUPER CHIEF is still what many believe to be no less than the finest train in the land. Once underway, passengers can choose between the 36-seat diner, with a menu of Fred Harvey cuisine, or the Turquoise Room, offering private dining for 12 in the Pullman-Standard Pleasure Dome lounge car. The luxury will last three more years. Then, like royalty made to mingle with commoners, the train will be consolidated with the all-coach EL CAPITAN.

(Don Ball Collection)

(Right) Shadows creep across the tracks as M.183 unloads express at the little station in Morton, Ill., just 12 miles from a 6 p.m. arrival at Pekin. On the first day of Spring, 1953, the motor is still holding down the Chicago-Pekin run. The 4-hour, 25-minute, 153.5-mile schedule, partly on the mainline, partly on the branch, calls for a brisk 38.5 mph pace, with stops. (J.J.Buckley)

30

(Above) The photographer has just arrived at Morton on a rainy March 24, 1953, when what to his wondering eyes should appear but a....well, what *is* that thing, anyway? Literally in a class by itself, 2611 is carried on the Santa Fe roster as a "transfer switcher" of the 2610 class. Rebuilt in the Topeka shops in 1948 from 1A, the "Andy" half of the original "Amos and Andy" EMC passenger diesels, the 1,800-hp two-engine unit is rated at a respectable 70,325 pounds tractive effort (compare with 89,560 for Alco's 1600-hp RSD4s). Assigned to California for a while, it has ended up in local freight service here on the Pekin branch. But it will not mu with anything else on the property, it is prone to breakdowns on the road, and, with a cab at only one end, it suffers from poor visibility. Engine 1, the "Amos" half of the duo, which was to have become the 2610, will instead be rebuilt into 83A, an E8m booster unit, in August. The 2611 will be sent to EMD in September, emerging as booster 84A, but still bearing its original EMC badge with construction number 536.

Headlight aglow, 2611 pauses amid switching chores in front of the depot.

Work at Morton finished, the unit heads back towards Pekin, a half-dozen freight cars and a way car tied to its homely tail.
(All, Sanford Goodrick)

Santa Fe Timeline

1954

+ Regular piggyback service offered for the first time
+ June 6: Santa Fe innaugurates the SAN FRANCISCO CHIEF, one of the last new streamliners to be put into service by any railroad
+ Total revenue: $545.3 million. Net income: $66.2 million

The **Chiefs**

BETWEEN CHICAGO AND THE WEST AND SOUTHWEST   Santa Fe

Headed by the *Super Chief* and *The Chief*, the Santa Fe great fleet of trains between Chicago and California offers a choice of fine accommodations to satisfy every taste and fit every pocketbook. And between Chicago and Texas, it's the *Texas Chief*. For smooth-riding comfort...friendly hospitality... delicious Fred Harvey meals...fascinating scenery...travel Santa Fe—*the Chief Way!*

(Below) Putt-puttering into the afternoon sun from the Lockport station, M.186 is 32.7 miles out of Dearborn and 5 miles from Joliet with #13, Jan. 30, 1954. The Chicago-Pekin motorcar trains were added to the schedule in 1931, and will continue until Oct., 1955. Then the three cars assigned to the run will move on to the 543-mile Wichita-San Angelo run, the longest motorcar run in the country.

(Gordon Lloyd, Lou Schmitz Collection)

(Above) Amid the comings and goings of the Warbonnet streamliner fleet at ancient Dearborn Station, Santa Fe still manages to work in its Chicago-Pekin motorcar runs. A little after noon on May 15, M.183 has arrived at Dearborn on #14 from Pekin. Now, coupled to a passenger car consist, it is being pulled back to the 18th Street for servicing.

(Below) A short time later, NW 2402 backs the M.186 down to the station for its afternoon departure on #13. The 1931-built motorcar is only six years older than the switcher. Both are Electro-Motive Corporation products. (All, J.J.Buckley)

(Above) At 1:35 p.m., M.186 sets out on its 153.5-mile journey. It's a warm afternoon, so the engineer has left the cab door ajar. The man standing in the open vestibule, possibly in violation of safety rules, might be the brakeman. Then again, with that red sweater, he might be a railfan from back east somewhere who stayed overnight in the YMCA hotel, the tall building in the background. The Y is a favorite with visiting fans, because it's cheap, clean, and close to the action.

(All, J.J.Buckley)

(Below) The new $4 million diesel shop at Argentine is so new on Oct. 17, 1954, that the big red SANTA FE sign has not even been hung up yet. Already, dozens of units are serviced and inspected here daily, and over the years the building will become a landmark to visiting railfans. Heaven knows how many near-collisions have taken place on Key Road Bridge just to the west as fans slowed their cars and craned their necks to take a quick inventory of the units on hand. This day, FTs, passenger F3s, and an NW 2 are on view.

(Don Ball Collection)

(Above) On the last day of the year, a set of passenger F7s, 330 in the lead, occupies a ready track at Argentine. It's hard to say which looks newer, the one-year-old diesel shop or the immaculately maintained five-year-old diesel set. A modeler's note: all that glitters is not stainless steel. Roofs, skirts, doors and ends of the Fs are painted aluminum.

Meanwhile, 10-year-old FTs soldier on. May 9, 1954, 116 idles at the Shopton, Iowa (Fort Madison) fuel racks. Though signs of steam have not been entirely obliterated at this division point, the railroad here has not seen an active steam engine since the Boy Scout passenger rush of 1953. *(Both, Lou Schmitz)*

(Above) The location is a bit of a mystery. That's unmistakably a Harriman Standard water tank in the distance, suggesting Mojave, where Santa Fe begins trackage rights on the Southern Pacific for the trek over Tehachapi. The occasion is a railfan special. Windows are open and, perhaps with a wink from the conductor, the photographer has swung open the Dutch door in the vestibule of the heavyweight coach to snap a few pictures. Despite the snow on the tops of the distant mountains, a rush of warm, dry desert air swirls in. A four-unit set of F3s with stock cars waits for the passenger train to clear. In the distance, a grove of trees—apparently the only trees for miles—shelters a section house. Hot, dry, barren, it's hard to imagine one railroad finding a reason to spike down rails here, much less two. And yet this is the gateway to California's San Joaquin Valley and its riches.

The photographer has not recorded the location or the date. But he has left us with a vivid image of a moment in desert railroading. (W.L. Heitter)

(Following page, top) Santa Fe's Chicago passenger engine facilities at 18th Street have been squeezed into a very small scrap of land for such a busy railroad—more than two dozen arrivals and departures a day. On this pleasant morning in June, 1954, almost every available track is crammed with engines, including an unusual E6A-E8B-E8A combination being hostled down to Dearborn station, and sets of PAs and F3s waiting to take out afternoon trains. The 2399, one of the steam generator-equipped RS1s the road acquired in 1947-49 to switch the coach yards, backs onto the turntable and a second RS1 idles beyond.

(Following page, bottom) An NW2 brings New York Central Pullman *Tri Borough Bridge* past 18th Street for a connection with THE CHIEF. Because of limited fuel storage capacity at the facility, strings of tank cars full of diesel fuel are always parked on one of the roundhouse leads or being switched out for fresh tanks. In three decades the scene will be almost unimaginably changed. A new skyline will have filled in the backdrop and Amtrak will have taken over such railroad passenger business as remains. (Both, Emery J. Gulash)

Santa Fe Timeline

1955

- 47 high-level cars ordered from Budd to re-equip EL CAPITAN
- Santa Fe offers to buy 236-mile Toledo, Peoria & Western for $10 million
- December 1: First train runs over new 48-mile Dalton Junction-Zacha shortcut to Dallas
- Total revenue: $593.3 million. Net income: $77.6 million

(Left) Waynoka, 106.6 miles west of Wellington, is the place where the 4-8-4s customarily drop off and the 2-10-4s carry on. Here, on July 7, 2920, one of three 2900s equipped with a twin sealed-beam headlight, lays over waiting assignment on an eastbound perishable. In just two weeks, the 2920 will head up WK-34 out of Wellington to Emporia, closing out steam operations east of Wellington. The next day, Aug. 1, she'll handle the last steam-powered freight over the Middle Division, a westbound empty refer drag. *(Don Ball Collection)*

(Above) The 2919, arriving form the west at Kiowa, Kan., is showing signs of neglect. Like lichen, rust is spreading across the smokebox front and the cylinders. She could use a paint job or a general cleaning. No matter. On July 26, the road-weary 4-8-4 is running off her last miles in revenue service. The Big Steam Show of 1955 is about over. Alco RSD7s are on order, and next summer when Santa Fe calls out a handful of steamers for Belen-Mountainair helper service the 2919 will not be among them.

(Clayton Tinkham, Lou Schmitz Collection)

(Left) The odds of catching steam on a freight out of Wellington, Kan., in mid-July, 1955, are pretty good, three-to-one, in fact, if you count the set of FT freighters led by the 174 that shares the ready tracks with three of the big 2900-series Northerns: the 2919, the 2922, and in the background, the 2906. In addition, the roundhouse is packed with road-ready Northerns — the 2917 and 2901 are visible — improving the odds. As early as late April, 1955, word went out on the railfan grapevine that Santa Fe was starting to recall steam from the deadlines. Even ancient 2-10-2s would be called up for switching service. By July, 86 steamers have been returned to work and as many as two dozen Plains Division freights a day are being dispatched behind steam. So it will continue until August 7. These engines have been freshly fueled and watered, and the sand domes have been topped off. Now the crew of the 2922 pauses for a moment to grin at the photographer before climbing aboard their charge. The only thing better than being here to photograph them would be to climb up and ride with them to Argentine or Waynoka.

(Don Ball Collection)

(Above) The picture looks a little brighter for 2-10-4 5021, even though at the moment she is in service on a lowly ballast train somewhere on the Pecos Division between Clovis and Belen. This is highly unusual. Unlike some other roads, which fritter away their remaining steam power on marginal assignments, Santa Fe is keeping its best engines for the annual perishable rush. And the 5011-series Texas types are unquestionably Santa Fe's best, capable of producing 93,000 pounds tractive effort and a maximum 6,500-hp horsepower at speeds over 35. Eat your hearts out, EMD and GE, with your SD90MACs and your DASH9-44CWs. *(Don Ball Collection)*

(Below) One of the ironies of the last days of steam is that the oldest 2-10-2s, the half-century-old 900s and 1600s, have survived to perform useful work while the 35-year-old 3800s and 3900s have all gone to scrap. At the start of 1955, these veterans had been retired and written off the books. But in April, as diesel switchers were called west to deal with bumper-crop harvests in California, they were written back into the books, dragged out of the storage lines and inspected. By June, 17 are under steam at Clovis, Belen, Emporia and here, at Amarillo, where the 1601 has been put to work. Their 74,800 pounds tractive effort makes them powerful switchers, ideal for kicking around long cuts of perishables and empty reefers. They will stay on the job through August and Santa Fe will finish out 1955 with 21 2-10-2s carried on the books, seven more than it started the year with.

(Below) Like a dinosaur suddenly come to life, the 1636 prepares to switch passenger cars at the Amarillo station. Smokebox painted aluminum, indicating that this was once a Gulf Coast engine, she is one of eight old 2-10-2s that will work here this summer. All have the high headlights and inboard trailing trucks that signify an older era in Santa Fe steam practices. *(Both, Lou Schmitz Collection)*

(Right) When is a PA not a PA? When it's been re-engined by EMD. In 1946, Santa Fe snapped up the original PA demonstrators, a purchase accompanied by rampant celebration and press agentry, because the lead unit was supposedly Alco's 75,000th locomotive. (It was, but only thanks to a bit of creative serial-number shuffling.) Numbering the set 51LAB, the road went on to buy a total of 44 PA1s and PB1 boosters over the next two years. They were exceptionally smooth-riding engines and turned in very good performances, for the most part, running like the wind over the flatlands and showing they could knuckle down on grades. Nevertheless, turbocharger blades snapped, crankshafts failed and the 2,000-hp units oozed oily, back smoke, a trait that later led rail historian and economist George Hilton to dub them "Honorary Steam Locomotives." And so in 1955, Santa Fe sent the 51LAB off to La Grange for installation of new 1,750-hp EMD 567 engines. The roof humps, easily visible, are the giveaway.

Here the trio hustles past 18th Street with Second #24, THE GRAND CANYON, returning from what is undoubtedly the first test run west. EMD's own test car is coupled behind the lead unit. The two-cycle EMD engines produce less smoke, but also, unfortunately, 250 less hp per unit, which is quite a lot when multiplied by three or four units. The remaining PAs will keep their Alco prime movers, though with improvements to the electrical system. Apparently happy with the result, Santa Fe will keep them around for at least 15 more years before trading them in—to EMD. *(Emery J. Gulash)*

(Right) As Bob Hope might say on his popular television show, How about that nose? If built as styled by Raymond Loewy, the Fairbanks-Morse 90 would have emerged from General Electric's Erie plant with a 15-foot prow. But FM's engineers prudently cut the design back by six feet. On a bright morning in 1956, 90LAB wait on track 5 in Los Angeles Union Passenger Terminal to take #72, the 7:45 SAN DIEGAN, down the Surf Line. Delivered to Santa Fe about the same time, and delivering the same 2,000-hp per unit as Alco's PA's, the Erie-builts are less successful. The opposed-piston engines suffer liner failures. Crankcases explode. While idling, oil accumulates in the lower cylinders, emerging in a spectacular cloud of blue smoke when they rev up. Deemed unsuitable for service to Chicago, the three-unit set found a home by the early 1950s on Los Angeles-San Diego runs, and occasional trips over Cajon to Barstow. *(Don Ball Collection)*

Santa Fe Timeline

1956

+ Power-hungry Pennsy leases 2-10-4s for Columbus-Sandusky, Ohio, service
+ New 29.5-mile branch constructed from Hysperia, near Cajon Pass, to serve Kaiser cement plant
+ Total revenue: $605.9 million. Net income: $70.2 million

(Above) On Sunday, Feb. 19, 1956, a contingent of railfans has descended upon Emporia, Kan., to ride #25, the "Little Ranger" behind motorcar M.131. Division offices are housed in the station here, accounting for the presence of one of the system's 50-foot office cars.

Nicknamed because it makes connections at both ends of its run with #5, THE RANGER, the motorcar will depart at 11:20 a.m., just five minutes after #5's arrival, then make its leisurely way down the mainline via El Dorado and Augusta to Winfield. If all goes well, #5 will just be pulling in at 2 p.m., having made the same journey the long way around via Newton. Purpose of the motorcar run is to deliver and gather up mail along the line and relay it to THE RANGER.

(Below) Right on time, THE RANGER has pulled up to the Emporia station behind passenger F7s for a brief stop. Most of the railfans are already on board the M.131, but two have stepped over to trackside to record #5's passage.
(Both, Don Ball Collection)

(Above) Earlier in the day at Emporia, the fans found FT 193 with two mates, looking almost as bright and shiny as the October day in 1944 when it emerged from La Grange (as the 153C). Santa Fe does take care of its diesels. With 402 idling nearby, the engine terminal here is a momentary mecca for FT fans. But the days of the FT are numbered. The railroad has 80 new diesels on order for 1956 delivery—mostly GP9s and F9s. In five years, after 17 years of service, the 193 will be returned to EMD as a trade-in on GP20 1138. (Don Ball Collection)

(Below) On Sept. 3, FT 427 and two boosters will soon put their collective 4,050-hp to work, muscling their westbound around Houlihan's Curve and up the hill to Edelstein. Three FTs is the usual power here. The combined 173,325 pounds tractive effort is fully equal to the 8-mile, 1.1 percent climb. Twice-renumbered 427 began life as the 106C, then became the 168C.

(Paul Stringham, William Volkmer Collection)

(Left) Santa Fe bought 59 H12-44s, and although they are a little top-heavy and tended to sway on uneven track, they are the dominant switching power on the road's east end and are well-liked by crews. On Oct. 14, 1956, the 7-month-old 555 is working Chillicothe, Ill., a crew-change terminal where its main duties consist of shuffling way cars and switching the nearby gravel pit. Sharp eyes will note the engine wears white stripes but aluminum numbers. (Paul Stringham, William Volkmer Collection)

(Above) The Quick and The Dead in 1956: The 5027 is one of five 2-10-4s that have been pressed into helper service out of Belen for the 1956 summer perishable rush. The big Texas and an F7 set have just gotten a train underway out of the Belen yards and across the Rio Grande, altitude 4,785 feet, but they'll soon have it up to 35 mph on the 41-mile pull to Mountainair, altitude 6,508. This is not like the great rush of 1955, when steamers seemed to be all over the place. But on July 2, 1956, it's the best show on the road.

(Jim Ehernberger, Lou Schmitz Collection)

(Left) Meanwhile, several hundred miles to the east back at Argentine, the storage lines are filled with rusting Northerns. A sad spectacle, the 3769 has probably not turned a wheel under its own power since late summer of 1953 when it was working freights between Argentine and Waynoka.

(Don Ball Collection)

And the 3768 has been idle since working the Clovis-Argentine pool that year. (Jack O'Donnell, Lou Schmitz Collection)

Santa Fe Timeline

1957

+ Fred Gurley retires and Ernest S. Marsh becomes president
+ August 27: 5021 and 3780 make final revenue steam runs on the Santa Fe
+ ICC approves joint Santa Fe-Pennsylvania purchase of TP&W
+ Total revenue: $626.7 million. Net income: $61.9 million

The Atchison, Topeka and Santa Fe Railway Company

63st ANNUAL REPORT

(Above and below) At 8 a.m. August 27, 1957, Engineer W.A. Riggs and Fireman L. Pelvland will climb aboard 2-10-4 5021 and set off down the Belen yards to help a 4-unit F7 set with an eastbound perishable up the grade to Mountainair. Northern 3780 will receive a similar call just an hour and 10 minutes later. Assignment completed, the 5021 will drift back down the pass and tie up at the engine terminal at 12:20 p.m. And at 1:30 p.m., the 3780, under the command of Engineer G.I. Riley and Fireman M.E. Key, will roll into the yards, closing the books on what historian Lloyd Stagner calculates as 88 years, four months and one day of steam locomotive operation on the Santa Fe.

The photographer has caught the historic duo resting between labors at Belen just a month before their final duty.

(Both Jim Ehernberger, Lou Schmitz Collection)

45

(Above) Motorcar M.117 arrived at Topeka at 9 a.m. on #55 from St. Joseph, Mo., and Atchison, Kan. She's been turned, fueled and inspected and awaits a 2:35 p.m. departure on #56, the run back up the branch. The schedule is in its last weeks, perhaps its last days. After a brief turn at freight service between Independence, Kan., and Ralston, Okla., later this year, the 29-year-old motor will be held for scrap. E8m 87, perhaps with THE CHICAGOAN, but more likely with a train of railfans who have come to ride the motorcar, occupies the adjacent track.

(Don Ball Collection)

(Above) The 87, one of several Santa Fe E8ms with aluminum frames around the number boards, has crossed the Missouri River into Atchison, Kan., with five heavyweight coaches and a baggage car. Clearly some kind of special movement is underway, because the 72.2 Atchison District hasn't seen regular passenger service, except for the daily-except-Sunday motorcar, for years. The high bridge at right carries U.S. 59 across the river, and just visible to the right of the track in the background, behind the radio tower, is the bridge-tender's shanty. Tracks at right belong to Missouri Pacific's Kansas City-Omaha line. For Santa Fe, Atchison is holy ground. It was here in 1860 in the office of one Luther Challis that a group of businessmen met to organize a railroad to connect Atchison, Topeka and Santa Fe following roughly the line of the Santa Fe Trail. Nine years went by before track was spiked down, and then it was to the south. It was only in 1874 that rails finally reached Atchison, and by then the little Missouri River town no longer figured in Santa Fe's transcontinental ambitions.

(Below) At 3:42 p.m., just as railfans are beginning to spread out with their cameras, Missouri Pacific E7 7004 swings into MoP's station with the northbound MISSOURI RIVER EAGLE. (Both, Don Ball Collection)

47

Santa Fe Timeline

1958

✚ January 1: THE SUPER CHIEF combined with EL CAPITAN, except in peak travel season

✚ February: Santa Fe slashes 24 hours from westbound freight schedules, permitting fifth-morning delivery for California points

✚ New "push-button" yard at Corwith completed

✚ Total revenue: $610.9 million. Net income: $67.2 million

The Atchison, Topeka and Santa Fe Railway Company

64th ANNUAL REPORT
for the year ended December 31, 1958

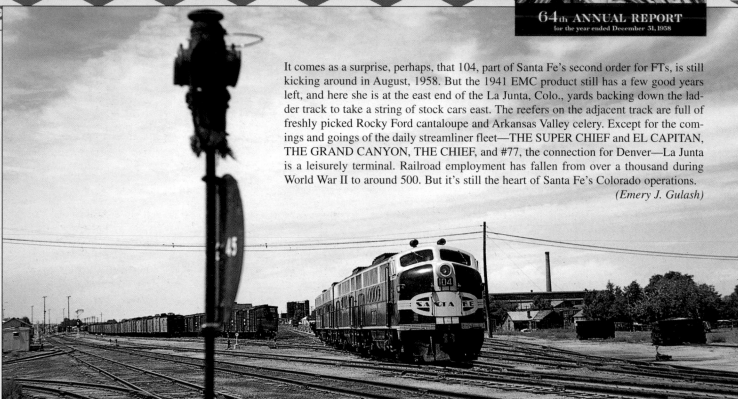

It comes as a surprise, perhaps, that 104, part of Santa Fe's second order for FTs, is still kicking around in August, 1958. But the 1941 EMC product still has a few good years left, and here she is at the east end of the La Junta, Colo., yards backing down the ladder track to take a string of stock cars east. The reefers on the adjacent track are full of freshly picked Rocky Ford cantaloupe and Arkansas Valley celery. Except for the comings and goings of the daily streamliner fleet—THE SUPER CHIEF and EL CAPITAN, THE GRAND CANYON, THE CHIEF, and #77, the connection for Denver—La Junta is a leisurely terminal. Railroad employment has fallen from over a thousand during World War II to around 500. But it's still the heart of Santa Fe's Colorado operations.

(Emery J. Gulash)

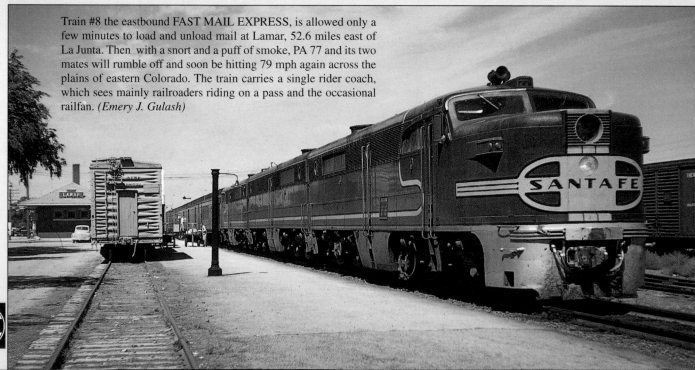

Train #8 the eastbound FAST MAIL EXPRESS, is allowed only a few minutes to load and unload mail at Lamar, 52.6 miles east of La Junta. Then with a snort and a puff of smoke, PA 77 and its two mates will rumble off and soon be hitting 79 mph again across the plains of eastern Colorado. The train carries a single rider coach, which sees mainly railroaders riding on a pass and the occasional railfan. *(Emery J. Gulash)*

(Above) A herd of zebras: Unlike Penn Central, Illinois Central and Norfolk & Western, Santa Fe somehow managed to turn black and white into an attractive diesel paint scheme, though technically RSD4 2105, idle in August, 1958, at Garden City, Kan., and the rest of the road's switchers and road switchers wear black and aluminum paint. The blue Santa Fe circle and cross, an emblem that dates back to 1901, is a nice touch. Interestingly, the chevrons point down on the long-hood end, up on the nose. (Emery J.Gulash)

(Right) An overnight February snowstorm, dazzling sunlight, and a black-and-silver paint scheme have combined to present exposure problems to the photographer. Nevertheless, here is a portrait of the 2800, one of 250 GP7s on the system, heading the eastbound local at Edelstein, Ill. This is about as bare bones a Geep as you can buy: no dynamic brake bubbles, no steam generator, no rooftop air reservoirs. (Monty Powell, Lou Schmitz Collection)

(Below) Santa Fe's two TR4 cow-and-calf sets, 2418AB and 2419AB, will spend virtually their entire careers in and around Argentine, where on June 8, 1958, the 2419AB is working the hump. The transfer version of EMD's 1,200-hp SW7, the units are a must-see for railfans visiting Kansas City, along with Santa Fe's famous one-of-a-kind GP7m 99, an FT cloaked in a GP9 body shell. In early 1979, the TR4s will be extensively rebuilt in San Bernardino, Cal. (Monty Powell, Lou Schmitz Collection)

(Above) Chillicothe lost its standing as headquarters of the Illinois Division to Shopton, Iowa, when the Illinois and Missouri Divisions were consolidated in 1956. But in February, 1958, freight crews still change here, way cars are shuffled and a small amount of local industry keeps a switcher or two busy. A-B-B and A-B-B-B sets of passenger F7s, led respectively by the 338 and 326, have just come down Edelstein Hill, 10 curves in 8 miles, and are headed for Corwith Yards in Chicago with an eastbound. (William Volkmer Collection)

(Below) On a considerably warmer day in August, the all-coach EL CAPITAN, makes a Chillicothe station stop. Passenger crews do not change here, so the streamliner will be rolling again quickly. Green flags fly from lead unit 43, an F7, indicating a second section, #18, THE SUPER CHIEF, is following. In the off-season, the trains are consolidated. Chillicothe's station, which once housed the Illinois Division headquarters, will burn down in 1963.

(Dick Wilhelm, Lou Schmitz Collection)

(Above) About two miles from a 12:05 p.m. arrival at Kansas City Union Station, train #212, THE TULSAN, rambles along the south bank of the Kaw, east of Argentine in August, 1958. The tracks have been raised and the river presumably tamed since the great flood of 1951. Tulsa-Kansas City #212 usually draws an E8m, such as the 81, or an E6 west of Kansas City.

(Don Ball Collection)

(Below) Beneath that amusement-park costume beats the heart of a real Santa Fe workhorse. Rails had just been laid over Raton Pass in 1880 when 2-8-0 132 was turned out—by Baldwin, of course. Twice renumbered, in 1898 as the 912 and in 1900 as the 2414, the engine lost its pilot wheels sometime early in this century to become an 0-8-0, in which arrangement she served for decades as the Argentine shop goat. In 1940, Santa Fe suddenly realized what it had right under its nose, and shop forces at Topeka restored the original number and rebuilt the engine to its original specifications: 19x28-inch cylinders, 51-inch drivers, 140 pounds boiler pressure, 23,600 pounds tractive effort. Soon renumbered once again, as the 1-spot, and named *Cyrus K. Holliday*, in honor of Santa Fe's founder, she was sent out on the publicity trail with two lovingly restored 1880-era coaches for just such occasions as the Burlingame, Kan., Centennial, May 17, 1958. It's also worth noting that the station here in Burlingame dates from 1869, when Santa Fe's rails were first spiked down here. Engine and exhibits will end up in the Kansas State Historical Society Museum in Topeka. *(Clayton Tinkham, Lou Schmitz Collection)*

(Above) Alco HH1000 2312 burbles past the Redondo Junction engine terminal with a transfer for Los Angeles' Hobart Yard, March 27, at an infamous location: On Jan. 22, 1956, RDCs DC 191 and 192 in SAN DIEGAN service entered the 15 mph curve in the background doing almost 70 mph, shot off the rails and wrecked catastrophically, killing 30 passengers and injuring 131. The 2312 now passing this way on a happier occasion will be around well into the 70s, when hundreds of railfans will make the pilgrimage out to Hobart to photograph the old Alco. By then, how many of those fans would give anything to photograph that almost-new GP9 in fresh zebra-stripes? And how many will suspect that 4-8-4 3751, parked on the next track, will live to steam another day? *(Alan Miller, William Volkmer Collection)*

(Below) Winslow, Ariz., was where dieselization began on the Santa Fe, the place where the 2-10-2s and 2-10-4s and 4-8-4s came off and the four-unit FTs went on for the long, dry pull across the desert to the Coast. In June 1958, a three-unit set of PAs waits to relay a westbound—most likely #7, FAST MAIL EXPRESS. The rows of refrigerator cars with open doors are being cleaned in preparation for the flow of fresh produce about to begin out of southern Arizona. *(Emery J. Gulash)*

Santa Fe Timeline
1959

✚ Santa Fe issues a new book of operating rules, numbered 1, ending the old 1894 numbering sequence with book number 101

✚ Santa Fe purchases the first of 30 new SD24s and 50 Alco RSD15s

✚ 4-8-4 2925 set aside for railroad's historic collection of motive power

✚ Total revenue: $651.6 million. Net income: $65.8 million

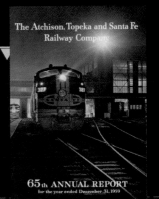

The Atchison, Topeka and Santa Fe
Railway Company

65th ANNUAL REPORT
for the year ended December 31, 1959

(*Above*) At 10:30 on a foggy March night along the Platte River bottoms, FT 105 rests at Colorado & Southern's Rice Yards engine terminal. Santa Fe doesn't have a place to call home in Denver, and so Burlington subsidiary C&S handles Santa Fe's switching chores and paper work here. In fact, some of the switchers are jointly lettered for the two roads. Though Santa Fe has been fully dieselized for almost two years, C&S has not quite managed that task, and a row of Burlington 2-8-2s loom in the darkness to the right. For several months yet, an occasional Mike or one of C&S's own 2-8-0s will shuffle up to the coal tower before heading off to its chores. (*Bill Marvel*)

(*Above*) On Sept. 29, 1959, something new is afoot at the Winslow, Ariz., fuel rack. SD24 931 is making its first trip west, in the company of slightly older sisters 906 and 904. With the turbocharger bulge in the side of the hood, they are harbingers of the second generation of diesel power to come, an ancestor of SD40s and SD45s. At 2,400-hp each, they would have astonished the men who pioneered on 1,350-hp FTs here, just as they will please the crew that draws them for the next westbound assignment. Santa Fe will go on to purchase 80 of the big units. (*Robert H. Leilich*)

53

(Above) The crew received a 6:30 a.m. call to take Extra 289C west from Winslow. It's a brilliant September morning with a slight chill in the air as the 4-unit set of F9s waits at the west end of the yard for the signal that will send it out onto the main. For the next several hours, she'll be grinding up a mostly 1.42% grade to Supai Summit before dropping down to Ash Fork, then starting the climb all over again to Seligman. The Third District of the Albuquerque Division is a grueling piece of mountain railroading. No wonder Santa Fe dieselized here first.

(Below) The fragrance of scrub cedar and junipers permeates the cab of 289C, throbbing along at a steady 35 mph, when at Winona #18, THE SUPER CHIEF, suddenly pops into view, just 15 minutes out of Flagstaff and, judging from the smudge of exhaust, running fast. She'll be by before you can blink an eye.

(Above) Just 4.4 miles further up the line, as the San Francisco Peaks rise into view at Cosnino, an eastbound freight tops the rise and comes rolling down the sag in a vain attempt to catch #18's markers. 12,670-foot Humphreys Peak, just ahead, is the highest spot in Arizona. It was once much higher. The San Francisco Peaks are all part of one broken mountain, an ancient volcano that blew its stack, Mount St. Helens fashion, hundreds of thousands of years ago. Santa Fe's builders had to construct much of their railroad through ancient lava flows. Flagstaff, largest city on the Santa Fe between Albuquerque and San Bernardino, lies at the foot of the peaks. The photographer, a management trainee with the Santa Fe, has nothing to do here but watch and learn, and he has the best seat in the house.

(Below) In a scene that soon will never be repeated, the 289C is climbing westward on the line out of Ash Fork when a reefer block suddenly appears from the west and glides across the crossover at Pineveta and down the grade. On the other side of the bridge, our train will turn north, travel up a short canyon, then reverse direction in a spectacular horseshoe curve and climb past Gleed, 567Cs shouting all the way. The eastbound will have easy work of it to Ash Fork. Then the real climb begins, the 1.85% to Supai Summit.

But in May Santa Fe announced plans to tame this operating nightmare, and even now crews are at work on a 44-mile line relocation that will take the rails north from Crookton to a point just east of Williams, with no grade steeper than 1%. The first train will pass over the new line Dec. 19, 1960. And this line will be abandoned shortly thereafter, leaving behind only the concrete bridge abutments, visible from old Route 66 east of Seligman.

(All, Robert H. Leilich)

(Above and following page) Otto Kuhler's work as a stylist of railroad engines remains controversial. A romanticist who wanted to bring the excitement and color back to railroading, Kuhler earned a name for himself in the 1930s by designing Milwaukee Road's famous Hiawatha streamliner, from the 4-4-2 all the way back to the observation car. He went on to create Baltimore & Ohio's streamlined Royal Blue, both 4-6-2 and train, and streamlined one of Southern's elegant 4-6-2s, a case of gilding the lily if there ever was one. Mostly, railroads called upon him to dress up old steam engines so that they could cash in on the big streamlining craze of the late 1930s.

His only diesel work of note was also Alco's first attempt at streamlining a locomotive, the DL-109 and its kin. There are enthusiasts who pronounce the results "rakish." Certainly the 50LA, seen here in profile and front view at Argentine, looked speedy: the pointed prow, the elongated warbonnet, those lanky Alco trucks that look like they were just made to lap up the miles.

But to other eyes, there is a sort of Art Deco-ish fussiness about the design. Little speed lines and tucks and creases have been stuck on where there is no need for them. The lower headlight, added by Santa Fe when a Mars light was installed, interrupts the slant of the front, then the centered number board above the windshield does it again. Perhaps 50LA's "good looks" were mainly a product of rarity and pure nostalgia. When Alco tried streamlining a passenger diesel the second time—the classic PA—it did better.

As for Otto Kuhler, that courtly, courteous gentleman retired to a ranch in Colorado where he spent his final years painting marvelous watercolors of steam locomotives, most of which were not streamlined. (Both, Don Ball Collection)

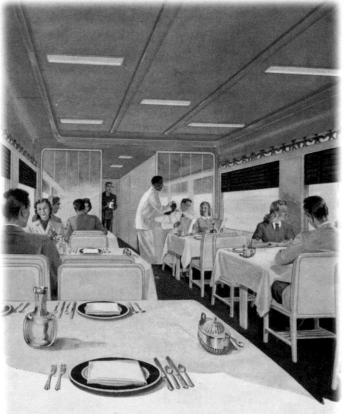

(Above) Aside from a railfan sighting into his twin-lens reflex and a railroad worker strolling down the platform, there is nobody in view to greet #5 as it rolls into Topeka at 9:50 a.m. or thereabouts, Nov. 15, 1959. The train, until recently listed in the timetable as THE RANGER, offers daily service from Kansas City to Dallas and Galveston, on the Gulf of Mexico.

(Below) A glowing signal and a derail warning sign protect #12, THE CHICAGOAN, as it switches from its own line to the tracks of the Kansas City Terminal Railway for the final lap into Kansas City Union Station, on Feb. 15, 1959. E6 13 and the two E8ms left San Antonio, Texas, yesterday morning and will not need fuel until Shopton, Iowa. After a 25-hour-run via Dallas, Fort Worth and Newton, #12 will pull into the station here at 12:05 p.m., some 20 minutes after the arrival of #212, THE TULSAN, via Olathe. The two trains will be consolidated and continue their eastward dash for an 8 p.m. arrival in Chicago. (Both, Don Ball Collection)

(Above) Coughing up the characteristic clot of black smoke, PA 73 and two mates are on the move again after a station stop at Topeka with #5, THE RANGER. The Topeka Transfer & Storage warehouse, a familiar landmark to visiting railfans, is in the background. Although most of Santa Fe's lucrative freight traffic bypasses Topeka on the Olathe line west of Kansas City, Topeka is still solidly a Santa Fe town. The railroad's general office building is right across the street from the state capitol, its largest shop complex is still busy with repairs to locomotives and rolling stock, and 10 passenger trains a day still arrive and depart.

(Below) Train #7, the westbound FAST MAIL EXPRESS, usually gets a four-unit F7 set out of Kansas City with a three-unit PA set holding down the run west of Barstow. But every now and then the train draws PAs in the east, as it has here at Newton, Nov. 15, 1959. Santa Fe has been carrying the U.S. mail into Newton since 1871, and in 1892 the road received the contract to carry mail 2,224 miles from Chicago to Los Angeles, first on the CALIFORNIA LIMITED, and starting in 1915 on #7. The PAs have their work cut out for them: #7 commonly runs to 24 cars, including express cars full of magazines and other priority shipments from the east, mail storage cars, a single RPO (three east of Kansas City) and, although the train hasn't been listed in the public timetable since 1943, a rider coach. Passengers are politely discouraged from taking the train. It's a tight 44-hour, 35-minute schedule with lots of stops, and no time to wait around for connections. (Both, Don Ball Collection)

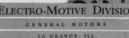

(Above) Corwith, Santa Fe's big Chicago freight yard, is oriented north-south, at right angles to the main line. This eastbound, about to bang across the Belt Railway of Chicago diamond at Nerska, has 1.4 miles to go before swinging south, crossing the Stevenson Expressway, seen in the background, and slipping into one of the receiving tracks at Corwith.

(Following page, top) Running on the Illinois Division—a good bet would be somewhere near Verona in the good, flat farmland between Streator and Chillicothe — 332-322-322B, a neatly matched F7 ABB combination, is hurtling westward with TOFC, a mode of traffic Santa Fe has been vigorously cultivating. In December, 1959, the surrounding fields sleep. But come spring, this is corn and soybean country.

(Following page, bottom) Climbing through lush mid-summer foliage, 328-328A-333A 308B are just about to top the short, winding climb out of the Illinois River Valley and emerge on the open prairie again at Edelstein. The F7s have replaced FTs here, just as they, in turn, will be supplanted by GP20s and U25Bs. And generations of railfans will continue to catch the changing scene from the old wooden bridge, and its concrete replacement, long after June 21, 1960 is a memory.

(All, Don Ball Collection)

1960

+ Santa Fe files application with ICC to acquire control of Western Pacific
+ December 19: First train passes over the new Williams Junction-Crookton cutoff in Arizona
+ Total revenue: $632.9 million. Net income: $51.6 million

The Atchison, Topeka and Santa Fe Railway Company

66th ANNUAL REPORT
for the year ended December 31, 1960

(Above) For a locomotive that was something less than a total success, Santa Fe has certainly gotten its money out of the PAs. On a spring afternoon in 1960, a pair still presents a noble sight on the head end of Second #24, THE GRAND CANYON, possibly near Lawrence, Kan. By now, other roads are edging their PAs toward the scrap lines or sending them in to EMD or GE as trade-ins on new freight units. But on the Santa Fe, the 67 and her sisters still find useful work. Even into the late 1960s, railfans can count on finding a brace of Alcos on the point of #23 or #24, or on #4, the southern route mail train. *(Don Ball Collection)*

(Below) Santa Fe's regular passenger business in Denver by July, 1960, is down to a single train, the daily connection for La Junta. So this must be a special, coming up the Colorado & Southern passenger connection for Denver Union Station. Rio Grande's Burnham coach yards are at left, and to the right, C&S's Rice Yard's Seventh Street engine terminal, which plays host to Santa Fe units in the Mile High City. Though it has been raining off and on, passengers aboard the special have enjoyed a spectacular view of the Rockies all the way up from Pueblo, 119.3 miles south. *(Ross Grenard)*

(Above) Two of Santa Fe's 250 GP7s, the 2807 and 2739, idle between branch-line assignments at Cushing, Okla., in late 1960. Shop forces have cut inspection holes in the side skirts of the 2739 for access to machinery. Otherwise, the two units are pretty much as delivered—in October and August of 1952, respectively. They will remain that way until the early 1970s, when Santa Fe begins rebuilding its GP7s, chopping the nose for better visibility, installing a solid pilot, and painting the renumbered units in the "yellow bonnet" scheme.

(Emery J. Gulash Collection)

(Below) GP7 2818, which left the Wichita station with mixed train #67 at 6:10 a.m., is arriving at Pratt with a single hopper and a 2410-class combine in tow at 10:15. The schedule allows only 15 minutes for work here. After dropping its combine at the depot, and switching out the hopper, the crew will execute a tricky "flying switch" to get the combine back on behind the geep for the return trip as train #68. (This unfolding drama will also be captured by the photographer with his 16mm Bolex movie camera and is included in the Green Frog video, *Santa Fe Odyssey I*) Arrival at Wichita is scheduled for 2:40 p.m. In June, 1960, the 33-year-old Wichita-Pratt run is one of 33 mixed trains still listed in the Santa Fe timetables. One more year will see the end of this interesting operation. (Emery J. Gulash)

Santa Fe Timeline

1961

+ 25 new baggage cars being built in Topeka shops
+ Skull Valley line relocation begun to reduce grades and curves on Arizona's Phoenix-Ash Fork Pea Vine
+ Santa Fe and U.S. Post Office conduct joint tests of containerized mail, Chicago to the Bay area
+ Total revenue: $621.7 million. Net income: $54.9 million

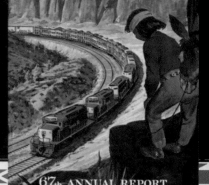

The Atchison, Topeka and Santa Fe Railway Company

67th ANNUAL REPORT
for the year ended December 31, 1961

(Above) The waiting room of the magnificent old Paris, Tex., station is boarded up. Passenger service from Dallas ended in the mid-1950s. And there hasn't been a regular motorcar run on the 100.5-mile branch since the war years. The M.122 is here to replace the Frisco 44-toner that formerly switched the joint Frisco-Santa Fe yards. In the past, Paris was an important interchange point. But by Sept. 16, 1961, traffic is down to a tri-weekly local out of Dallas.

(Right) Reequipped at Cleburne shops with footboards and a backup light, the 75-foot RPO-smoker-coach is remarkably spry, kicking around cars of produce for the Campbell Soup factory and of East Texas lumber. Its service here will end in September, 1962. Then the car will sit at Cleburne until it is sent away for scrap in October, 1963.

(J.J. Buckley Collection)

(Right) Also finishing out its years pulling freight cars, M.118 rests behind the Wellington, Kan., roundhouse. From here, it sallies forth weekdays to run mixed trains to Geuda Springs, Anthony and Harper. (Robert E. Bruneau)

(Above) The 18th Street Bridge over the east end of Argentine Yards affords several photographers a splendid panorama of the railroad, the river and the distant skyline of Kansas City late this March, 1961, afternoon. A few minutes past 5:25, here comes E8m 83 with #211, THE TULSAN. One of Santa Fe's Fairbanks-Morse H12-44s, the 529, waits for the five-car streamliner to clear AY Tower.

(Below) Five minutes later, the 529 has returned to her chores as #11, THE KANSAS CITYAN noses into the setting sun behind a smoking E6A-B duo. The two trains run combined east of Kansas City, and when they split, the Big Dome lounge goes to #11 while #211 gets the round-end observation car. The daily departures and arrivals to and from the west, almost always within a few minutes of each other, is one of the most satisfying rituals of Kansas City railroading. *(Both, Don Ball Collection)*

(Above) Having come down the 193.7-mile "Pea Vine" from Ash Fork in the small hours of Sept. 28, 1961, train #47 has the whole day to cool its wheels in Phoenix before setting out at 5 p.m. as #42, for the return journey up the branch. The train, which will run until 1968, carries a baggage car, 44-seat coach, diner-lounge, and sleeping car from the connection at Williams Junction. The Pea Vine, formerly Santa Fe, Prescott & Phoenix, exists primarily to serve one of Arizona's richest produce-growing regions.

(Right) GP7s outnumber GP9s five to one on the Santa Fe. And the 730 is just one of six GP9s equipped with steam generators for passenger service. Unlike the GP7s, all GP9s got dynamic brakes. The railroad has been repainting the zebra-stripped engines in yellow and blue since 1960.

(Both, Lou Schmitz)

(Below) On Oct. 15, 1961, GP20s 1129-1138-1139-1131, stopping for a crew change at Chillicothe, Ill., are the very latest thing on Santa Fe rails. Two of the units rolled out of EMD a month ago, the other two were built in August. Santa is buying its GP20s in two batches, 25 in 1960 and 50 this year, trading in FT cabs and boosters to EMD. Assigned to the Illinois Division because they are equipped with cab signals, they seem to be taking over, and it's getting rare to see anything else on east-end freights. The engines that introduced turbocharging to main line freight service, they will become the 3100-series in the 1969-70 general renumbering and, rebuilt as GP20u's starting in the late 1970s, will run right on into the 1990s, never owing the railroad a nickel. (William Volkmer Collection)

Santa Fe Timeline

1962

✛ Orders placed for 24 new Hi-Level chair cars
✛ March: Completion of Skull Valley line relocation
✛ Clovis yard modernized
✛ Total revenue: $630.2 million. Net income: $70.7 million

The Atchison, Topeka and Santa Fe Railway Company

68th ANNUAL REPORT
for the year ended December 31, 1962

(Right) Baldwin DS4-4-1000 2287—the 4-4 is for the B-B wheel arrangement, the 1000 for horsepower—idles in the Clovis, N.M., yard, 1962. Though Baldwin was Santa Fe's favorite steam builder, it didn't fare as well with its diesels. Eddystone works started building DS4-4-1000s in 1949, five years after turning out its last steamer for Santa Fe. They were an improvement over the earlier VO1000 diesel switchers, getting 1,000-hp out of a six-cylinder turbocharged engine, where the VOs required eight cylinders. Santa Fe bought 41 and was satisfied. But aside from a couple of centercab transfer units, it turned to other builders for its diesel road power.

(Below) Railfan-photographers Donald Duke and Stan Kistler coined the term "diesel mice" for the 44-ton switchers that Santa acquired because, by agreement with the unions, any locomotive heavier than 90,000 pounds required both a fireman and an engineer. Parked in front of Santa Fe's elegant Colorado Springs station July 28, 1962, GE centercab 464's duties consist mainly of a little light switching and swapping out a sleeper, slumber-coach, chair car, and cafe-lounge from the Rio Grande's daily ROYAL GORGE which handles the Colorado Springs section of Burlington's DENVER ZEPHYR between here and Denver. The little engine will eventually be sold to Kansas City's Board of Public Utilities.

(Both, Lou Schmitz Collection)

67

(Above) Did any locomotive wear EMD stylist Leland Nickerbocker's warbonnet scheme as handsomely as Alco's PAs? And did any of the other paint scheme that graced the 297 PAs Alco built look as good as Santa Fe red, desert yellow, and acres of stainless steel of the Warbonnet? Fortunately, steam builder Alco resisted the temptation to "style" the PA, opting for a clean, crisp design. That long nose, unspoiled as yet by MU receptacles, offers engine crews extraordinary protection in case of collision. Even the curved fairing above the cab windows is functional, channeling runoff during rainstorms. The 52, the fourth PA delivered to Santa Fe—in 1946, at a cost of $187,000—pauses briefly in August, 1962, at Richmond, Cal., on the point of #2, the SAN FRANCISCO CHIEF. (*Lou Schmitz Collection*)

(Below) The Mother of All PAs, 51LAB, makes a station stop March 25 with #74, one of the SAN DIEGANS, at Fullerton, Cal. On the adjoining track, #23, THE GRAND CANYON, will continue on to Los Angeles, but #74 will leave the Los Angeles Division here, turning south on the Fourth District "Surf Line." In 1960 F7s began suffering frequent boiler failures on the 123-mile San Diego run, and PAs were assigned, usually in pairs. But the 51 and her mates, re-engined with EMD 567 engines, deliver 250-hp less per unit than the Alco-powered versions. Although some rewiring has improved performance, Santa Fe still deems it necessary to assign three to a train. (*Leo Calota, Matthew Herson, Jr. Collection*)

(Above) By 1962, Santa Fe is starting to thin the ranks of the FTs, sending them in on trade for GP20s. But you'd never know it from this southbound at Temple, Tex., in July, powered by no less than nine of the original freighters, led by 411. The FTs lack MU receptacles in the nose, and therefore the two sets of power have separate crews. Temple is headquarters of the Southern Division, which by 1962 encompasses virtually all Santa Fe trackage south of Fort Worth, and Fs of all models still reign supreme here. Even so, the 411 faces retirement in a year. (Lloyd Keyser)

(Right) Near Mormon Yard in Stockton, on California's Valley Division, F7A 204 leads a pair of GP7s on a southbound. The unit is the 12th of 462 F7s acquired by Santa Fe, its most numerous diesel class. They represent a 150-hp jump over the 1,350-hp FTs, and, with their improved D-27 traction motors, a marked improvement in tractive effort over their immediate predecessor, the F3.

(Steve Bogen)

(Right) The 185L, laying over in Denver's Rice Yards in May, 1962, wears an F7 grill but is otherwise a standard FT. Denver is another terminal where fans can occasionally encounter one of the old freighters. Unlike the 411 seen earlier at Temple, the 185L can count on two more years of employment before being traded in to EMD on a GP35. (Matthew Herson, Jr.)

(Above) Alco's RS1, the original road switcher, enjoyed the longest production run of any American diesel locomotive, from 1941 to 1960. Santa Fe waited until 1947 to buy its first, and went on to buy eight more. Essentially S-2 switchers with a short hood that could house a steam boiler, all but one were assigned to passenger switching duties between 18th Street and Dearborn, where the 2399 is at work May 30, 1962. The ninth works in the Los Angeles area. The 2399 will be traded to GE for a U36C in 1973.

(Below) The 2398 retrieves a Railway Express Agency car at 15th Street Tower, just south of Dearborn, on July 8, 1963. The 42-foot 7-inch refrigerator express 6686 is one of 194 former troop sleepers converted and leased to REA by Chicago Freightcar Leasing.

(Both, J.J. Buckley)

Santa Fe Timeline

1963

+ Santa Fe and other western carriers hit by national freight car shortage in the fall
+ Diesel maintenance facilities in Kansas City and Barstow enlarged
+ Santa Fe considering use of nuclear explosives to excavate new bypass between Goffs and Ash Hill, California
+ Total revenue: $636.8 million. Net income: $67.8 million

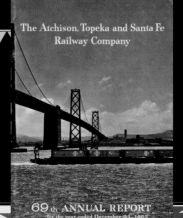

The Atchison, Topeka and Santa Fe Railway Company

69th ANNUAL REPORT
for the year ended December 31, 1963

(Above) The RS1s were not the only diesels the Santa Fe acquired for passenger switching. In 1956, the road added FM H12-44TS 541-543 to the Dearborn fleet. As with the RS1s, the short hoods housed a steam generator for heating passenger cars during switch moves. The three-of-a-kind units lasted long enough to be leased to Amtrak in 1971 to switch its Chicago coach yards. Two of them, including the 542, seen here with a cut of nine cars near 18th Street on May 30, were scrapped. But the 543 ended up in the Santa Fe's collection of historic motive power, and, oddity of oddities, is on display today in Sacramento, a gift to the California State Railroad Museum.

(Below) Climbing out of the dip at Chicago's 16th Street Crossing, F7 39C is inbound on May 30 with the nine cars of #16, the TEXAS CHIEF. About a mile south of Dearborn, 16th Street Tower guards the crossing of Michigan Central and Illinois Central's St. Charles Air Line with Rock Island and New York Central's approach to LaSalle Street Station. Santa Fe, running on Chicago & Western Indiana track here, passes beneath. The Chicago River lift bridges are in the background. This is one very busy place, what with Rock Island's twice-daily commuter rush, still-lively passenger business on the New York Central, Santa Fe, Grand Trunk and Erie-Lackawanna, plus transfers on IC, Chicago & North Western and Milwaukee Road. (Both, J.J. Buckley)

(Right) On June 21, 1963, after spending most of the past decade in branch-line service in Kansas, Oklahoma and Texas, M.115 has come to Chicago to be the Belle of the Ball. First of the 1929 75-foot RPO-smoker-coach gas electrics built by the Electro-Motive Corporation, the largest single class of motor cars on the Santa Fe, she has been invited to the 30th anniversary celebration of GM's Electro-Motive Division, EMC's successor. Cleaned up, painted, the M.115 waits at Corwith. Alas, like Cinderella, she won't be invited. Someone will remember that the 34-year-old car was reequipped, by Topeka shops in 1951, with a new D-397 Model diesel engine —by GM rival, Caterpillar. And there is no Fairy Godmother at hand. In two years, the M.115, once the first, will become the last of its class to be scrapped.
(J.J. Buckley)

(Below) The M.190 has fared much better. Arriving at Roswell, N.M., Aug. 15, 1963, she is a regular on the Santa Fe's last motorcar run, trains #25/26 between Clovis and Roswell. Delivered in 1932 and designed to pull five cars in mainline service at speeds up to 80 mph, "Old Pelican," as she has come to be called, was Santa Fe's only three-truck articulated motor, a 900-hp wonder that, when the V-12 Winton was properly tuned and timed, could deliver a remarkable 50,050 pounds tractive effort. Although a failure in mainline service, the experiment educated both maker EMC and Santa Fe, who went on to collaborate on the successful 1 and 1A passenger units two

years later. As for M.190, after kicking around the system on various main line and branch line runs, she was dressed up with a little makeshift streamlining and a warbonnet paint scheme in the mid-50s and sent to the Clovis-Carlsbad run. With a round-end observation coach tied to her tail, she is capable of 60-65 mph and alternates with the M.160, also gussied up in the warbonnet scheme, almost until #25/26 are discontinued in 1967. The M.160 will go to the Age of Steam Museum in Dallas. The M.190 will end up in Sacramento as part of the collection of Santa Fe curiosities at the California State Railroad Museum. *(William Volkmer Collection)*

(Above) What other railroad in December, 1963, is not only running 24-year-old passenger diesels, but running them proudly, in the service for which they were intended, and looking almost as good as when they made their debut? (Okay, besides Colorado & Southern's E5s on the TEXAS ZEPHYR.) One half of Santa Fe's E3 roster suns itself outside the Argentine diesel shop in the company of an E8m booster and cab. The trio probably came in a little past noon on #12, THE CHICAGOAN—where, in November, 1938, she made her break-in runs—and will go out this afternoon, most likely on #11, THE KANSAS CITYAN. The trucks could use a touch-up of aluminum paint, but with its slanted nose and sleek good looks, the 1938 EMC product still looks twice as fast standing still as almost anything else on the railroad does moving. And she still has five years of service ahead of her before both cab and booster are traded in to EMD on F45s. (Lou Schmitz Collection)

(Below) At 7:55 a.m. Aug. 11, 1963, train #7, the FAST MAIL EXPRESS, has just pulled into Kansas City Union Station behind E3 11, and E8m booster and E6 15, its usual power out of Chicago. The train has several cars of New York- and Chicago-Kansas City express, mail storage cars and two RPOs to drop off. Then it will collect the westbound express and mail storage cars, pick up a Kansas City-Los Angeles RPO, and at 9:04 a.m. be on its way again behind four F7s. The photographer's overlook from the Broadway Bridge at the west end of the station provides a good view of the rooftop fins Santa Fe has installed on the E3 and the E6 to break up the airflow and create turbulent air that will cool the radiator exhaust, which tends to run hot in these units. (William Volkmer Collection)

(Above) Santa Fe, which had never been particularly fond of Alco products in the days of steam, liked the builder's diesel switchers very much, purchasing over a dozen years 70 S2s, two S1s, and 38 S4s. The latter were assigned to various California points, such as San Bernardino, where the 1518 wears a new coat of paint. The railroad has been repainting switchers and road switchers into the blue and yellow scheme since early summer, 1960.

(Right) Trains Magazine in its August 1960 issue reported that the new paint scheme was the railroad's response to critics who thought the zebra-stripe too austere. As if to put the matter to a test, the power assignment office has brought together on November 2, 1963, in Chillicothe, Ill., the old and the new schemes as applied to two otherwise identical Fairbanks-Morse H12-44s. Both schemes look fresh in the bright sunshine. The 515 wears the classic black and aluminum, with the blue Santa Fe cross insignia. You be the judge.

(Right) Sister 512 wears the new scheme. Both have the distinctive Raymond Loewy-designed carbody with roof overhang and slightly slanted nose that graces early H12-44s. Santa Fe purchased 62 FM switchers between 1945 and 1957, assigning most of them to territory east of Argentine. All will be off the roster by 1974.
(All, Lou Schmitz Collection)

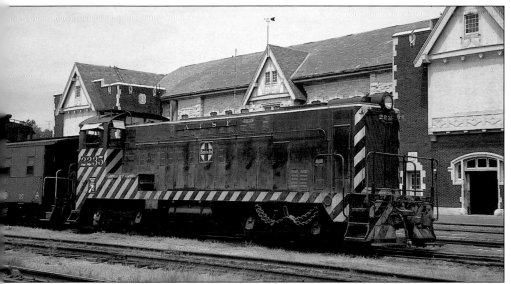

(Above) Sending up what must be an enormous racket, 2273 and 2291 work the Clovis, N.M., yard back-to-back on Aug. 15, 1963. The 41 turbocharged Baldwin DS4-4-1000s, delivered in 1948 and 1949, were among the last locomotives Santa Fe would ever purchase from old friend Baldwin. They are ubiquitous between Argentine and Albuquerque, and down into Texas on the Southern Division, and the railroad has fitted a few of the 2260-class with MU connections specifically for service here.

(Left) Santa Fe bought more VO1000s than any other railroad, 59 of them starting in 1939 and continuing through the World War II years when it pretty much had to accept what the War Production Board assigned it in the way of motive power, or do without. The 2235, in front of the Emporia, Kan., station, was an adequate switcher for its time, but by August, 1963, its time is about over. The engine has escaped the "four hole" exhaust stacks that the builder installed on some VO1000s to correct an overheating problem in the early one-hole version. (Both, William Volkmer Collection)

(Left) Ordered from Baldwin almost simultaneously with the DS4-4-1000s, Santa Fe's nine DS4-4-750s are powered by a non-turbocharged 750-hp prime mover. The builder reportedly put those tall exhaust stacks on the switchers because Santa Fe's Baldwin-built 4-8-4s wore stack extenders. Still dressed in stripes in Topeka, Aug. 11, the 633 will exchange its stripes for blue and yellow by spring. The box on the roof just in front of the cab houses a radio with built-in platform antenna, a Baldwin invention. (Lou Schmitz Collection)

(Above) Those Texas Fs! Leading a freight south towards the Missouri Pacific diamond at Fort Worth's famous Tower 55, dual-service F7A 337, at the head of an A-B-B-A combination, could just as well be heading up the TEXAS CHIEF in a day or two, illustrating the versatility that led Santa Fe to keep on buying the 1,500-hp freighters until it had acquired ten percent of EMD's total production run. By then, the F7 had been superseded by the F9. (Santa Fe bought 36 of those, too.) Located on the edge of downtown Fort Worth within walking distance of both the Santa Fe and old Texas & Pacific stations, Tower 55 is one of those places where the clan gathers, because sooner or later everything passes here. Besides Santa Fe and MoP, fans in April, 1963, can expect to see trains and transfers of the Katy, Rock Island and Southern Pacific and its two subsidiaries, Cotton Belt and Texas & New Orleans. Santa Fe's shops at Cleburne, 30 miles south, is the maintenance base for 248 of the F7s and GP7s, which explains their frequency on this line. In December, 1974, Cleburne will transform the 337 into CF7 2488 as part of its massive F-unit rebuild program.

(Below) At the modest engine facility just south of its Fort Worth station, Santa Fe FT 140L awaits assignment in April, 1963. Both A-units in the set, 140L and 140C, have escaped the first big purge of FTs in 1960-61, when a batch of the units were traded in on GP20s, and the great purge of 1962-63, for GP30s. But in just one year, they'll both go in to EMD in trade on GP35s. (Both, K.B. King)

(Above) Around noontime in summer, things can get pretty hectic south of Raton. First, there's one or more sections of #23, THE GRAND CANYON, plus, once a week, a special for tour groups that is dispatched out of Chicago Sunday mornings and runs close to #23's schedule. Then there are separate coach and sleeper sections of #17, THE SUPER CHIEF-EL CAPITAN. No sooner has the last of the westbounds passed and you have #24, THE GRAND CANYON eastbound, coming at you. And everything is flying down this semaphore-signaled single track at 79 miles an hour. On Aug. 23, 1963, under creamy New Mexico clouds, First #17, the all-coach EL CAPITAN, is flying green flags indicating there's more to come. The countryside is surprisingly lush for this late in the summer. (Bill Marvel)

(Left) In 1892, Santa Fe offered to transport renowned artist Thomas Moran to the south rim of the Grand Canyon if it could have the pick of anything he might paint there for advertising and promotional purposes. Moran, who had first visited the Canyon in the 1870s with Maj. John Wesley Powell's expedition, gladly accepted. Traveling to the Canyon by stagecoach from Flagstaff, he painted this masterpiece. In 1895, the road's traffic manager W.F. White began sending out thousands of full-color lithographs of the work, in gilt frames, to hotels, schools, and "anywhere that there was a fair chance of the picture bringing in business." Santa Fe finally bought the 40-by-30 inch canvas for its own collection in 1912, and continued to reproduce it on calendars as late as 1982, when passenger service to the Grand Canyon was a memory.

(Left) Santa Fe has been taking trainloads of tourists to the Grand Canyon since Sept. 17, 1901. But by September, 1963, traffic is down to #14/15, the single daily train up and down the 64.3-mile branch. This late in the season, there is a distinct chill in the air, and passengers who have spent the day exploring the Canyon's South Rim will be grateful to get on board #14 for the 8 p.m. departure for Williams Junction, where the chair car and two sleepers will been handed off to connecting trains. Combine 2545 has been assigned to the Grand Canyon run for years. The tour trains out of Chicago will run four more seasons, and #14/15 will last until the summer of 1968. Then Santa Fe will drop all service, leaving its most famous on-line attraction to be overwhelmed by swarms of buses and private automobiles.

(Howard Fogg)

(*Above*) Dynamic brakes whining in the sharp air of a November morning, GP30 1215 and three sisters drop down the grade from Arizona Divide with a westbound at Maine, Ariz. Some 18 miles west of Flagstaff, Ponderosa pine and the snowy 12,670-foot summit of the San Francisco Peaks dominate the scene.

(*Previous page, top*) Silhouetted at dawn at Ludlow, Cal., Nov. 24, 1963, five GP30s led by 1227 take a westbound across the Mojave. Desolate little Ludlow was once quite a railroad town, terminus of the 8-mile Ludlow Southern, which is remembered, if it is remembered at all, as the road that tried to hitch up the running gear of an ancient 4-6-0 and a Hart tractor motor, and the storied Tonopah & Tidewater, which ran 163.07 miles north to Beatty. Both were gone before World War II.

(*Previous page, bottom*) At 6:30 a.m., according to the photographer's notes, 1227 and its train is four miles west of Ludlow. A green board beckons eastbounds. (*All, Howard Fogg*)

(Above) The first of Santa Fe's 75 GP20s, 1100 leads an eastbound into Chillicothe, Ill., in low afternoon light, Nov. 2, 1963. Rebuilt at San Bernardino shops in November, 1980, the 1100 will still be on the roster, albeit under another number, in the late-1990s, a career spanning almost four decades. Few steam engines managed that.

EMD's GP20 was the outgrowth of an experiment on Santa Fe's rival, Union Pacific, which in 1955 applied Garrett AiResearch and Elliot turbochargers to 19 of its GP9s. The turbochargers, by forcing air into the cylinders under pressure, allow a greater burn of fuel, increasing the power of the basic 567 prime mover. EMD, which had resisted turbocharging the 2-cycle 567, was impressed and began offering the 2,400-hp SD24, with a turbocharged 16-cylinder 567D, in 1958. It was also the first road switcher with a lowered nose for visibility. The 2,000-hp GP20 came shortly afterwards. The builder did well with the units, selling 260. (Lou Schmitz Collection)

(Below) And yet another string of the GP20s rolls in behind the 1105. Santa Fe's practice is to send out its GP20s and the newer GP30s in solid sets. Mix-and-match will come later.

(Dick Wallin, Lou Schmitz Collection)

The turbocharger stack is visible just behind the forward radiator fan housing of 1107, also arriving in Chillicothe on Nov. 2.
(Dick Wallin, Lou Schmitz Collection)

Santa Fe Timeline

1964

- ✚ SAN DIEGAN service reduced from five to four round trips a day
- ✚ Entire 143-mile Winslow to Seligman line now double-track
- ✚ May 7, Santa Fe begins to eliminate firemen in freight and yard service
- ✚ Total revenue: $659.9 million. Net income: $72 million

The Atchison, Topeka and Santa Fe Railway Company

70th ANNUAL REPORT
for the year ended December 31, 1964

(Above) Excess power is evidently being transferred east as 1139 heads up a whopping 16,000-hp, 8-unit set of GP20s, Oct. 31, 1964. To assemble the equivalent horsepower, the motive power dispatcher would have to send out a dozen FTs—or four SD70MACs. Chillicothe's extensive sand and gravel operation, a eyesore but an important source of online traffic to the railroad, is visible in the background. *(Dick Wallin, Lou Schmitz Collection)*

(Below) Freshly arrived in the engine terminal at Bakersfield, Cal., Aug. 2, 1964, GP35 1346 is likely on its first run on the Valley Division, having been delivered by La Grange only two months ago. The 2,500-hp unit faces an unhappy future: Renumbered 3346, she will be rebuilt as a GP35u in late 1982 only to be written off after a wreck at Pico Rivera in Los Angeles, Jan. 28, 1988. *(Alan Miller, Lou Schmitz Collection)*

(Above) There is no way for a railroad to get into or out of the Los Angeles Basin without climbing over mountains. And the severest climb is Santa Fe's 2.2% grade over Cajon Pass. Having almost completed the haul from San Bernardino (elevation, 1,077 feet), F7A 19C and four mates are bringing #20, THE CHIEF, through the curving cut at the west end of Summit (3,823 feet). Back in the lunch counter-diner, the crew has cleared up after the late lunchers and is catching its breath before the first call for dinner. On an exceptionally clear afternoon in November, 1963, riders in #20's fulldome bar-lounge are being treated to a breathtaking panorama of the San Gabriel and the San Bernardino Mountains.   (Matthew J. Herson, Jr.)

(Right) Five GP30s, led by 1268, bring a westbound into Summit. The grade from Victorville is a relatively benign 1.6%, but the 2,250-hp units have had a workout. Within ten years, everything in this picture will be utterly transformed. Santa Fe will lower and completely rearrange its line at Summit and Southern Pacific will have built its own line over Cajon, the Colton-Palmdale Cutoff, along the hillside in the background.

(L. Calloway, Bob Wilt Collection)

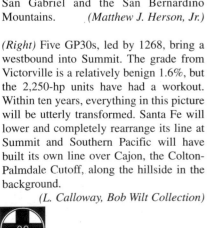

(Above) Though they burn oil in the cylinders rather than in a firebox, the new generation of motive power at San Bernardino still need plenty of sand to keep their footing on Cajon's 2.2%. The veteran sandhouse has served everything from 4-6-0s to 2-10-10-2s over the years, and in October, 1964, is providing grit to almost-new GP30s 1239, left, and 1270, right. RSD15 848 heads up a trio of 4-year-old Alco Alligators at left.

(Below) The 849, just in off the hill, leads a freight through the San Bernardino yards. Former Alco demonstrator DL600, the 849 is the final RSD15 purchased by Santa Fe. In 20 years, in what would at first seem to be a backward step, the shops in the background will replace the 2,400-hp Alco 241 engines in three of the 800s with 2,000-hp EMD 645s. Paired with slugs, the resulting CRSD20 hybrids will be used in hump yard duty just over the hills in Barstow. (Both, Lloyd Keyser)

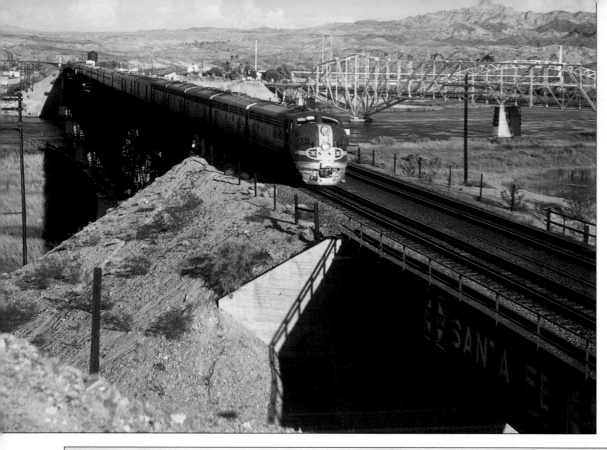

(Left) Always sensitive to light and atmosphere, the late Howard Fogg has noted that the temperature at 5:17 p.m. Sept. 12, 1964 is 110 degrees as train #19 comes rolling across the 1,500-foot Colorado River Bridge from Topock, Ariz., headed for a stop at Needles, Cal. This is the third bridge to carry trains across the waters here. The first, upstream, disappeared before the turn of the century. The second is visible at right. Until 1945, Santa Fe rails crossed over, swung along the river bank towards the left, and passed below the photographer's position, beneath that overpass with the Santa Fe sign, then continued upstream to Needles. Frequent flooding on the Colorado finally forced the railroad to build this high bridge. After it was completed, the old cantilevered bridge carried Route 66 across the water. (Howard Fogg)

Flanked by a few sandblasted palm trees, a telephone shelter, and a location sign, appropriately-named Bagdad is little more than a siding in the heart of the Mojave where the railroad can park a few water cars. But in its day, this was a helper station, dispatching engines for the push west up Ash Hill and on to Barstow. March 15, 1964, the rails are burnished by the passage of SD24 924 and four mates with an eastbound. Few railfans get out this way, where daytime temperatures can reach 125. The men who built the Southern Pacific line through here (soon traded to Santa Fe for some Mexican trackage and a little cash) must have been in the grip of some heat-induced whimsy when they named two equally desolate locations up the line Yukon and Siberia. (Howard Fogg)

(Above) At Griffith, Ariz., where the Mojave ends, the tracks separate for a 10-mile passage on opposite sides of the dry wash through narrow Kingman Canyon. Turning to follow the eastbound line, SD24 940 and two companions have been climbing the 1.42% grade steadily since leaving the Colorado River at Topock, and still face a long uphill battle. In steam days, the 149.7-mile line from Needles to Seligman was the longest helper district in the country.

(Below) As the sun sets behind the motels and used car lots of Kingman, 940 blasts past the station and heads east toward the seven-mile straightaway across Walapai flats. The engines get a short respite here, then the climb resumes. Kingman was named in honor of Lewis Kingman, the wiley and energetic Santa Fe engineer who, under cover of darkness the night of Feb. 26, 1878, put his construction crews to work grading the line up Raton Pass, thus beating rival crews of Denver & Rio Grande, who were sleeping back in Trinidad. *(Both, Howard Fogg)*

(Right) The photographer has pulled off Interstate 40 at exit 211, as countless railfans have done over the years, and followed Winona Road to the overpass, where he is in time to catch the 803 at the head of three Alligators burbling westward with an equally divided consist of stock cars and tank cars.

(Below) The view west from Winona Road is one of the most spectacular on the Santa Fe. After passing through the sweeping curve at darling, the Alcos will be pointed straight at Flagstaff and at the San Francisco Peaks, the shattered remnants of an ancient volcano. The surrounding countryside is covered by an extensive lava flow and pocked by cinder cones, many of which are being mined for road-building material and railroad ballast.

(Both, Howard Fogg)

(Above) RSD7 611 and an RSD5 lead #53, the daily freight down the "Horned Toad" from Albuquerque, into Smeltertown, on the northwestern edge of El Paso, June 27, 1964. Southern Pacific's Sunset Route is up the embankment to the right, and the Rio Grande River and dusty hills of Mexico to the left. By the mid-1960s, the 2,400 hp RSD7s can be found almost anywhere from Denver to El Paso and west to La Junta, usually traveling in the company of one of more of the RSD5s. *(Bill Marvel)*

(Below) Having climbed out of the Rio Grande Valley, GP30 1283 brings empty refrigerators across the straightaway west of Dalies, N.M., where the northern line via Raton and Albuquerque rejoins the southern line via Amarillo and Clovis. The photographer is standing on Pietown Bridge, an original Route 66 overpass. Just a mile or two down the road is the Wild Horse Mesa Bar, a cool, dark and reputedly dangerous refuge on a hot summer afternoon where they will, nevertheless, take a railfan's money in exchange for a cold beer. *(Howard Fogg)*

(Right) Small pockets of snow still lie in the shade beneath the piñon trees on March 17, 1964, as 33L, a passenger F3A, brings #20, THE CHIEF, east for an 8 a.m. stop at Las Vegas, N.M. The train has four more years to run before it is dropped from the schedule in May, 1968, by cost-cutting Santa Fe.

(Below) Engines attended to in Las Vegas, #20 is on the move again, splitting the semaphores near Wagon Mound at the authorized 79 mph. The landmark, visible in the distance, was named by travelers on the old Santa Fe Trail who thought it looked like a covered wagon. The railroad is replacing semaphores with target signals, but the old signals will linger a few places along the Colorado Division into the 1990s.

(Both, Howard Fogg)

(Above) By Dec. 18, 1964, the Christmas rush is well underway, and Santa Fe has been running many of its trains in two and even three sections for the past week. First #17, EL CAPITAN, flies green flags for THE SUPER CHIEF, which will be following along shortly, near Gallinas on Raton Pass. The grade is 2% here, but in a mile or so F7A 41 and its mates will have to really dig in on the 3.5% to the top.

(Below) Santa Fe kept an operator stationed at Hebron until 1954, when the Koehler mine closed down. But demands for Raton coking coal reopened the mine in 1958, and the area is experiencing something of a coal renaissance. Koehler is shipping 2000 tons a day, enough to fill 40 of those hoppers creaking along behind the 600. And the mine is also processing a little coal trucked over from a new development in York Canyon to the south. Within two years, rails will reach up that canyon and coal trains will come rumbling down to the mainline four times a week for Fontana, ending 60 years of operations at the Koehler mine.

(All, Bill Marvel)

At one time, a network of branch lines fanned out to gather coal from mines in the Raton area. But in December, 1964, only the 14.5-mile line to Kaiser's Koehler Mine is still active, as RSD7 600 brings its train down to the junction with the main line at Hebron. The loads will be taken 10 miles north to Raton, where they will be picked up by the evening westbound and forwarded to Kaiser's plant at Fontana, Cal.

89

(Above) At the south end of the Joint Line, the paired Santa Fe and Rio Grande lines north to Denver, the yards at Pueblo, Colo., have always been a good place to catch varied motive power. Left to right, on a November afternoon, 752-A at the head of a Fort Worth & Denver (Burlington) F7 set, Santa Fe 265C on a similar Santa Fe set, and RSD5s 2128-2162, power for the local freight to La Junta. By agreement, Colorado & Southern freights are manned by Santa Fe crews on the joint line. *(Ross Grenard)*

(Below) Consist swollen with Christmas mail and express on Dec. 17, 1964, #201, the La Junta-Denver connection, pulls up to the brick platform at Fowler, Colo., behind E8m 81 and a mate. The train left La Junta at 1:05 p.m., shortly after arrival of #20, THE CHIEF, from the east. As #190, it will return this evening, arriving back in La Junta at 11:50 p.m., in time to catch #19, THE CHIEF westbound, at 12:33 a.m. The connection will run right up to the eve of Amtrak in 1971, three years after THE CHIEF will have been dropped from the schedule and there is nothing left to connect with. *(Bill Marvel)*

(Right) RSD5 2135 trundles along near Avondale, 16 miles west of La Junta, with #61, the local freight for Pueblo, on Dec. 17. Missouri Pacific's Pueblo-Kansas City line parallels Santa Fe rails here a couple hundred yards to the right. At Avondale, a spur runs north to serve the vast Pueblo Army Depot and, by the end of the decade, the U.S. Department of Transportation High Speed Ground Transportation Test Center.

(Bill Marvel)

(Above) With a familiar EMD drone, M.190 departs Carlsbad, N.M., with the "Pecos Valley Chief," as local wags call it, otherwise known as #26 to Clovis. The three-truck articulated motorcar took over the run from boiler-equipped GP7s several years ago and seems to be giving satisfactory service. Originally equipped with a distillate-burning engine, it received a standard 900-hp EMC 567 diesel at West Wichita in 1949. The front section carries the diesel, the second houses the baggage compartment, and so a coach is added to accommodate passengers. On July 4, 1964, a former roundend observation car, one of two assigned to #25/26, brings up the rear. (Below) Located in the middle of a vast potash- and sulphur-mining region, Carlsbad in 1964 frequently dispatched strings of RSD4s and -5s to switch long lines of hoppers on one of the numerous mine spurs and industrial spurs. The 2141 sets out from La Huerta Yard with a caboose and a single hopper. (All, J.J.Buckley)

The third car regularly assigned to the run and sole remaining roundend, 1940 Pullman-built 3197, waits at the Carlsbad station for its morning departure to Clovis behind the M.190. Like M.160, the motorcar that alternates with M.190 on the schedule, 3197 will end up at The Age of Steam Museum in Dallas' Fair Park.

(Above) With a clatter and a cloud of smoke from four 2,000-hp 244 engines, #2, the SAN FRANCISCO CHIEF eastbound, gets under way at Gallup, N.M., on Sept. 25, 1964. Until #1 and #2 were inaugurated in 1954, Santa Fe offered no through service to The Bay Area, and the two streamliners have become highly popular with travelers. Since May, the train has been running with hi-level coaches, 1955 equipment bumped down from EL CAPITAN, which has brand new hi-levels. That smoke coming from the PA is caused by turbine lag, a situation in which the exhaust-powered turbocharger struggles to keep up with increasing fuel consumption as the engines accelerate. (Don Ball Collection)

(Below) Train #1, the SAN FRANCISCO CHIEF westbound, departs Amarillo amid a cloud of dust and oil smoke behind PA 54 on June 2, 1964. Unlike the rest of the streamlined fleet, the San Francisco streamliners follow the southern route via Clovis and Belen. A Kansas City-Oakland containerized mail car leads the consist. This 1962 innovation will not, however, prevent the U.S. Post Office Department from canceling most railroad mail contracts in 1967.

(Don Ball Collection)

(Left) Coming into the home stretch, F7A 45 brings #4, the Southern District mail train, down the four-track straightaway to Kansas City Union Station. All that remains, in the fall of 1964, of the once glorious CALIFORNIA LIMITED, trains #3/4 now hustle the U.S. mails from Gallup to Kansas City, combining at either end with #7/8, the MAIL AND EXPRESS. The train typically carries connecting cars for Missouri Pacific. But while interesting, that is not what the photographer has come here for today. Dimly visible in the far background, just where the Kansas City high line swings down to bring trains of Union Pacific and Burlington into the station, is Chicago, Burlington & Quincy 4-8-4 5632. Painted gold earlier this year for the centennial of that railroad's Chicago-Aurora service, the O5 Northern is in town for a fan trip.
(Don Ball Collection)

(Below) Still in business at the old stand, FM H12-44TS 541 brings the equipment from this morning's #20, THE CHIEF, up from Dearborn Station to 18th Street for servicing. On March 1, 1964, the 8-year-old switcher has managed to escape the blue and yellow paint scheme. *(J.J. Buckley)*

(Preceeding page) The fuel rack at Argentine offers one-stop service—fuel, sand, water on a quick turn-around. PA 77, just off #4, the Southern District mail train from Gallup, has come up from the station. It's 4:30 p.m., and in the next few hours, workers will inspect and service the units, perform minor repairs, and replenish the supply of drinking water in the cab before sending them back down to the station in time for 10:50 p.m. departure on #1, the SAN FRANCISCO CHIEF. This has been, for several years, the standard ritual for the Kansas City PAs, and in October, 1964, the visiting railfan can pretty much count on finding at least one set of the units laying over during daylight at Argentine. (Bill Marvel)

(Above) At four minutes after 9 a.m., just as workers all over the city are settling into their daily routine, PA 65 begins its day at the head of #7, the westbound MAIL AND EXPRESS, easing out of Kansas City Union Station. Typically, #7 will carry four cars of express off the New York Central at Chicago destined for Los Angeles plus a car to be dropped off at Barstow for Richmond; at least one mail storage car for Richmond and several for Los Angeles; an LA RPO; another block of mail storage cars and express for Richmond via Barstow; and, bringing up the rear, a 2602-class rider-express coach. The latter are a source of some discontentment among railroaders who ride the train. They are drafty and uncomfortable and before the end of the year, the road will send them to the shop for rebuilding and assign standard heavyweight coaches to the train.

(Left and above) Begrimed after its 1048-mile dash from Gallup, the 77 and its mates await attention. (Bill Marvel)

95

(Below) Santa Fe acquired 20 FM H16-44s in 1951 and '52, and by April, 1965, all are working between Argentine and Topeka, St. Joseph, Emporia, and the line out to Superior, Nebraska. The photographer has arrived at Holiday Junction early in the morning to catch 3018 and 3012 hustling past with the daily local for Topeka. The 1600-hp units have a reputation as fire-starters and will be traded in to GE within three years.

(Above) The top-heavy H12-44s are supposedly restricted to 35 mph, but 539 is doing at least 45 as it kicks up a dust cloud east of Holliday with the way freight for Leavenworth. About 11 miles west, the train will leave the Topeka line at Wilder Junction, cross the Kansas River and, at Bonner Springs, the tracks of the Union Pacific, and continue north on the leisurely 27-mile branch. *(Both, Bill Marvel)*

(Above) In a rare quiet moment, the morning lineup awaits the call at Chicago's cramped 18th Street engine facility. First out will be power for THE CHIEF, which leaves Dearborn at 9:05. In the following 14 hours, 18th Street will dispatch power for six departing trains, and service and inspect power from five arriving trains. The discerning eye will detect subtle differences among the three sets of Fs lined up this June morning. F7 44L, left, and F3 33C, center, are painted in the regular F-unit Warbonnet scheme, for example, while F3 16L, right, still wears the E-unit scheme in which the curve of the bonnet extends back past the second louver. The 16L also has retained the raised radiator fans of early F3s. The 33C will be traded in on a SD-39 in 1969. The other two will be transformed into CF7s at Cleburne. *(Don Ball Collection)*

(Below) The Chicago RS-1s are not only used in passenger switching. Here, on Sept. 25, 1965, the 2395 and a way car set out near 21st Street to retrieve some freight cars from lineside industries on Chicago's near south side, including, perhaps, the big Cuneo Press plant in the background. The placard on the side of the way car admonishes employees to "Watch Out for Axy Dent." *(J.J. Buckley)*

100

(Above) By the mid-1960s, the PAs are still regularly assigned to SAN FRANCISCO CHIEF, the mail trains and most Surf Line trains. PA 75L has been seeing some hard use and the 18-year-old engine shows it as she waits in Los Angeles Union Passenger Terminal to take another SAN DIEGAN down the coast. Evidently the forces at Redondo Beach have not been keeping up the usually meticulous maintenance standards. *(Don Ball Collection)*

(Right) Barstow is headquarters for PA maintenance, which explains the presence of 64 at the diesel shop on Sept. 8, 1965. Though five feet shorter than EMD's competing E-units, the PAs look longer, with that six-foot nose—like looking out at the railroad over a ping-pong table—and those lanky 15 1/2-foot trucks with their idler axles. Although Southern Pacific owned more PAs—52 to Santa Fe's 44—the handsome passenger engines have come to be associated more closely with Santa Fe than with any other railroad. Santa Fe has the second-largest fleet, and, until Delaware & Hudson purchases a quartet of ex-Santa Fe PAs, it will have the last. All will be stored by 1968.

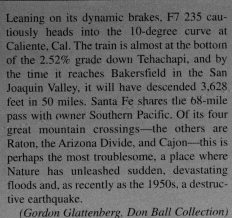

(Right) Speaking of long noses, also awaiting work at Barstow today is RSD15 826. This Alligator will return here for good, albeit in highly altered form. In 1976, Santa Fe will replace the Alco 251 prime mover with an EMD 645C, renumber the unit 3901, reclassify it as a CRSD20, mate it with a slug, and put it to work on the Barstow hump. Two other RSD15s will be similarly transformed. They will last until 1983.

(Both Carl Hehl, Lou Schmitz Collection)

Leaning on its dynamic brakes, F7 235 cautiously heads into the 10-degree curve at Caliente, Cal. The train is almost at the bottom of the 2.52% grade down Tehachapi, and by the time it reaches Bakersfield in the San Joaquin Valley, it will have descended 3,628 feet in 50 miles. Santa Fe shares the 68-mile pass with owner Southern Pacific. Of its four great mountain crossings—the others are Raton, the Arizona Divide, and Cajon—this is perhaps the most troublesome, a place where Nature has unleashed sudden, devastating floods and, as recently as the 1950s, a destructive earthquake.

(Gordon Glattenberg, Don Ball Collection)

(Above) Richmond is the end of the line, Santa Fe's terminus in Northern California. Rails reached the shores of San Pablo Bay here and stopped in 1900. A ferry took freight and passengers on to San Francisco. In 1904, passenger trains began running to Oakland, 11 miles south. But Richmond has remained the center of Bay operations. In August, 1965, the view of this busy terminal from the old wooden walkway across the yards takes in the Standard Oil Refinery and the engine terminal, until 1955 site of a 21-stall roundhouse. The three-unit PA set is power for the SAN FRANCISCO CHIEF, whose consist can be seen beyond. The switch at left foreground takes the line down to Berkeley and Oakland.

(Below) Looking to the east, the diesel shop, concrete power house, and metal car repair building are visible across the tracks.

(Both, Robert Leilich)

(Above) The tower casts a long afternoon shadow across the Amarillo yards in December, 1965. Headquarters of the Western Lines and the Plains Division, Amarillo is mostly a place where crews change and trains are swiftly relayed to their destinations. Diesels at the servicing facility, far right, may be laying over between runs up to La Junta, Colo., or down to Slayton. The remnants of the 28-stall roundhouse, the 100-foot turntable and the shop complex are beyond. The grain elevators in the distance mark the Rock Island's Memphis-Tucumcari and the Fort Worth & Denver lines east of town.

The long wooden building houses the car repair shop.
(Both, Robert Leilich)

(Previous page, top) Santa Fe's trains from the east reach Pueblo from La Junta, then turn north to follow the busy Santa Fe-Rio Grande Joint Line to Denver. But originally, Santa Fe wanted to continue due west from here, right up into the Rockies to tap the rich mining regions. The Denver & Rio Grande, still stinging from its defeat at Raton Pass, was already at work west of Pueblo, and the inevitable result was the Royal Gorge War, in which workers (and hired thugs) from both sides posted forts and even fought a few pitched battles. The conflict was settled in court in Rio Grande's favor—it was, after all, the home road. In November, 1965, Santa Fe still maintains a branch west a short distance to Canon City. But the Rockies belong to the Rio Grande, whose joint Pueblo facility with Missouri Pacific is at left. Santa Fe and Colorado & Southern's joint yard is at right. (Robert Leilich)

(Previous page, bottom) Taking on a few last minute express shipments at Pueblo Union Depot, Oct. 30, 1965, Santa Fe #201 has appointments to keep. The La Junta-Denver connection will return this way again, as #190, at 10:45 p.m. The magnificent old red sandstone station, a fine example of Romanesque Revival architecture, was designed by a Chicago firm and completed in 1890. Unfortunately, the original 150-foot clock tower was lowered by 30 feet after the building was damaged in a flood. But the station will remain long after the last passenger train has passed this way, a thriving restaurant-retail-apartment complex. (Matthew Herson, Jr.)

(Above) Once rowdy Dodge City, Kan., where in 1876 cowboys fresh off the Western Trail filled the saloons and Bat Masterson and Wyatt Earp patrolled the streets, is a much quieter town by June 3, 1965. The 1897 station, which once housed El Vaquero, a fine Harvey House Hotel, still fronts on Wyatt Earp Boulevard. But the action is behind the station, where #7, the FAST MAIL EXPRESS, is loading mail and express for points west. The 19C pulled in at 2:35 p.m. and is scheduled to leave at 1:40 p.m. Between arrival and departure, however, the crew will have reset their watches from Central to Mountain Standard Time. (Emery J. Gulash)

(Above) Snow-capped Pikes Peak in the background, Alco road switchers lead a La Junta-Denver freight on the Joint Line's north track at Pring in October, 1965. Just ahead, the short but vigorous climb up Monument Hill to the divide at Palmer Lake.

(Below) At Monument, the work begins in earnest. The next five miles will tax the pulling powers of the RSD7-RSD5-RSD7 combination.

(Below) The 600 and its mates approach the top of the grade. These rails will remain bright and busy right up to the day in mid-1974 when they are taken up to eliminate some Colorado Springs grade crossings. Only the southbound line, visible at right, will remain to handle the long parade of coal trains, empties and helper movements that will in a few years clog up a once-fluid stretch of railroad. *(All, Bill Marvel)*

(Above) In the first weeks of July, 1965, the Flood of the Century has struck northern Colorado, playing havoc with rail operations. Denver has been cut off from the east, and Rock Island trains are detouring to Colorado Springs, then turning north on the Joint Line, which has itself been washed out in several places. By July 13, the line has been patched together, permitting Santa Fe to send the 2139 through, northbound on the southbound track at Spruce, with local #98 from Pueblo.

(Below) The photographer would not have believed it had he not witnessed it himself: Four railfans have stopped for a bowl of chili in Fowler, in the Arkansas Valley west of La Junta. Now, just east of town they have come upon this local freight headed for Manzanola with a set of rattling old work cars on the head end. The lone RSD5 is poking along at 35 mph. As the car of railfans pull alongside however, the Alco starts to accelerate—past 40, then 45, 50, 60. At 70 mph, they drop back, mouths agape. A later check of the employee timetable shows that the Alcos are indeed allowed 70 mph on this line. Still, the 2159 was shading it a bit. (Both, Bill Marvel)

(Left) We are at Williams Junction, Ariz., at the east end of the 1959-60 Crookton line change. The PAs on #8, the eastbound FAST MAIL EXPRESS, are waiting for the westbound freight behind the 1205 to clear the crossovers beyond the signal.

(Below) The objects hanging above the tracks in the distance are switch heaters, a very necessary piece of equipment here in the Arizona high country where blinding blizzards and freezing temperatures are not uncommon three or four months out of the year.

(Left) Behind the mail train, an eastbound powered by a GP30-GP35 quartet waits at the Williams Junction station, built to accommodate passengers changing trains for the Grand Canyon and Phoenix. Williams itself is three miles west on the original mainline, which now runs only as far as Ash Fork and a connection with the Pea Vine for Phoenix. Everything else now takes the cutoff, a superbly modern piece of high-speed double-track railroad where no grade is steeper than 1% and freights are allowed 70 mph.

(All, Howard Fogg)

(Above) Train #1, the SAN FRANCIS-CO CHIEF, has made its stop at Stockton, Calif., and now is coming across the single-track Middle River drawbridge, 15 miles west of town in the marshes of the San Joaquin Delta. Eastbound counterpart, #2, has been waiting. Soon, with the characteristic clatter of four-cycle engines, the PAs will ease forward and the SAN FRAN-CISCO CHIEFs, eastbound and westbound, will be on their way to their destinations. *(Robert H. Leilich)*

109

(Above) After the 49-mile cutoff from Dalton Junction to Dallas opened in 1955, Santa Fe briefly ran separate Dallas and Fort Worth sections of the TEXAS CHIEF. But there wasn't enough business, so the train now runs combined as far as Gainesville, Tex., where an intricate set of maneuvers splits the train into a main section for Fort Worth and Galveston and a short plug run to Dallas. Shortly after 3 p.m., in August, 1965, #16 from Fort Worth pulls into North Gainesville Yard behind F7A 43C.

(Above) Shortly afterwards, the train has been split just in front of the diner, *Awatobe*, and #116, the Dallas section, which has been waiting, backs down with a sleeping car, two coaches and baggage car.

(Below) Gainesville Shuffle completed, GP7 2886 knits the combined train back together. Soon the engineer will get the highball and #16-116, 22 cars long, will be on its way to Oklahoma City, Kansas City and Chicago.

(All, Lloyd Keyser)

(Above) What Horseshoe Curve is to Pennsy and Sherman Hill is to Union Pacific, Raton Pass is to Santa Fe—its most famous, and most arduous mountain crossing. Sure, there is Cajon and Tehachapi. But Cajon is shared with Union Pacific, and the tracks over Tehachapi belong to Southern Pacific. The Pass of the Rat is Santa Fe's own, six miles of grinding 3.5% (7 miles of 3.3% for east-bounds). In December, 1965, #20, THE CHIEF, rounds the great curve at Wooton Ranch and drifts down the grade toward Trinidad. Here, after he sold his toll road over the pass to the Santa Fe in 1878, mountain man Uncle Dick Wooton retired to build his ranch house, sit on the porch and watch the trains go by.

(Right) Warm and snug in the cab of #20, just outside of Trinidad, Robert Leilich, a management trainee on the Santa Fe and the son of former Western Maryland vice-president George Leilich, knows that west-bound Second #17 will be coming into view at any moment. The all-coach section of THE SUPER CHIEF-EL CAPITAN is running late behind 37C.

(Right) Next up, waiting in the siding at Thrasher behind a set of PAs, is #23, THE GRAND CANYON, head-end swollen with Christmas mail and also running late.

(All, Robert H. Leilich)

Santa Fe Timeline

1966

+ National airline strike June 8-August 15 temporarily boosts passenger revenues
+ September 28: York Canyon coal line dedicated
+ Total revenue: $728.8 million. Net income: $93.4 million

The Atchison, Topeka and Santa Fe Railway Company

72nd ANNUAL REPORT
for the year ended December 31, 1966

(Above) Headed south through a wet spring snow that has fallen overnight, April 4, 1966, the 266L is on the Joint Line just south of Denver with gondolas full of scrap iron for the Colorado Fuel & Iron mill in Pueblo. The highway alongside is, appropriately, South Santa Fe Drive. The grill-less 266L will be rebuilt in October, 1972, as CF7 2599. *(Bill Marvel)*

(Previous page, top) In early 1966, the FTs are retired, but most of the 462-unit F7 fleet remains active. Cleburne, Tex., has become the maintenance base for Santa Fe's remaining Fs, so the ABBB set here is getting plenty of care. Starting next year, a number of the F7Bs will be gutted, packed with radio equipment, and sent out as control cars for master-slave operations. The following year, having pondered the future of its F-unit fleet, Santa Fe will begin a massive new program here at Cleburne in which 233 Fs will be rebuilt into 1,500-hp CF7 road switchers. The 276L will enter the shops in March, 1974, and emerge as the 2529. Eventually passed along to several terminal railroads and short lines, it will still be active in the mid-1990s.

(Previous page, bottom) There are minor differences between units. The 204C, heading an AABBA set at Clovis, N.M., in July, lacks the lifting lugs attached to the nose of 276L. It will go to Cleburne in May, 1971, and, as the 2638, eventually be scrapped by Santa Fe.
(Both, K.B.King, Jr.; Ed Seay, Jr. Collection)

Something new to
remember
every
magic mile

There's so much to see... so much to do... so many comforts to enjoy, that you'll never forget your trip through the colorful Southwest on any one of Santa Fe's five famous trains between Chicago and California

Santa Fe

Super Chief-Chief-El Capitan
Grand Canyon-California Ltd-

R. T. ANDERSON, General Passenger Traffic Manager, Santa Fe System Lines, Chicago 4

Mad dogs and railfans go out in the August sun on Cajon. The photographer is longing for a cold 7-Up, but it would be a shame to come all this way and miss the passage of the 47L as it leads First #20, THE CHIEF, through the cut at the west end of Summit. Green flags indicate a following section, most likely the weekly train of Grand Canyon tour groups.

(Bill Marvel)

(Above) Knock on the door of the Santa Fe operator's house at Summit, and there's a good chance on this January afternoon in 1966 that relief operator Chard Walker will open it, introduce himself, extend a hand, and give you a lineup of impending movements over Cajon. To start with, #23, THE GRAND CANYON westbound, is just coming up behind F3A 33C. By the end of the day there will be at least eight Santa Fe passenger trains and perhaps two dozen freights over the pass, plus Union Pacific traffic. Walker might also give you a brief tour, pointing out the track behind his home where, in steam days, pushers cut off passing freights and parked the way car. When they were safely out of the way, the brakes would be released and the way car would roll back down the slight incline to (everyone hoped) gently couple back on to the rear of the train. It was a deft maneuver, performed by men who had perfected their skills in years of experience. *(Matthew Herson, Jr.)*

(Below) Coming up the west side of the pass near Alray, just below the first tunnel, seven units strain to lift an eastbound up the 2.2% on Cajon, August 7, 1966. One GP30 is rated at 1,350 tons here, and there are three GP30s, two GP35s, an RSD15 and a GP7 on this train. Alray is easily accessible from the old highway, which runs beneath an overpass. Eventually, Interstate 15 will leap over the tracks here, and Alray will have lost much of its remote, out-of-the way atmosphere. *(Bill Marvel)*

(Right) The future has much in store for PA 59L, which, in May, 1966, at Los Angeles' Redondo Junction engine facility, appears to have be out-of-service but freshly shopped. In December of 1967, Santa Fe will sell 59L and three sisters for $30,000 each to Delaware & Hudson, whose president, F.C. "Buck" Dumaine, Jr., is something of a railfan and wants to run the engines on THE LAURENTIAN and MONTREAL LIMITED. When Amtrak takes over, the two trains will be dropped, and the former 59L, now numbered 16, will be leased to an excursion company for a short time, taken back by D&H, and sent to Morrison-Knudsen in Boise for a new 2,400-hp Alco prime mover. It will return to work Amtrak passenger trains, occasional freights, and even a few Boston area commuter runs. Then it will be leased to the National Railroad of Mexico, where it will be used and abused and finally stored under frightening circumstances at Empalme.

(Alan Miller, Matthew Herson, Jr. Collection)

115

(Previous page, top) Robert Leilich, who is out seeing the Santa Fe, has taken another of his terminal panoramas. The view to the southeast from the street overpass near the north end of the yards at Belen, N.M., takes in the yard office and 17-stall roundhouse, which in February, 1966, still houses 4-8-4 2925 and 2-10-4 5021. Ten years or so ago, the photographer might have caught them working their last seasons, helping eastbound perishables up Abo Pass through a gap in those distant mountains.

(Previous page, bottom) Belen is the center of Santa Fe's New Mexico operations, the crux of the Horney Toad line between Albuquerque and El Paso, and the east-west transcontinental freight line. Looking south over the 28-track yard, the El Paso line is at right. Just beyond the wreck train left of center is the icing plant, capable of taking on a 90-car train at a time during the annual perishable rush. To the left of that is the 120-foot turntable, with a couple Alcos parked beyond. In the distance, the line to Clovis curves and crosses the Rio Grande River to begin its climb. *(Both, Robert H. Leilich)*

(Below) Ten years after they were wrecked at Redondo Junction, RDCs DC-191 and 192 have been rebuilt and are working #13/14, the El Paso-Albuquerque runs, where for the time being they have replaced an E8m. Pausing northbound at the Belen station, they make the demanding 504-mile round trip in 14 hours, leaving Albuquerque at 6 and arriving at El Paso at 11:40 p.m., then setting out at 8 the following morning for a 1:45 p.m. arrival in Albuquerque.
(J.J.Buckley)

(Above) Clovis is where the Great Plains end and the long saw-tooth climb west begins. The town owes its existence to the Santa Fe, which created a division point here when it constructed the Belen cutoff in 1903-07. The view west from the tower takes in the once-bustling roundhouse, at left, and the rip track, where refrigerator cars made obsolete by mechanical refrigeration are being scrapped out. The repair tracks and yards are to the right. The line south to Carlsbad and Pecos, Tex., leaves the main line beyond the highway overpass in the distance. The complex of buildings on the horizon is Cannon Air Force Base.

(Following page, top) The Clovis turntable, which once turned dozens of 4-8-4s, 2-10-2s, and 2-10-4s a day and sent them back out on the road, gives a lone Baldwin DS4-4-1000 a leisurely ride before it takes the local freight down the line to Carlsbad. The lead F7 of a two-unit set pokes its nose out of the roundhouse. This is cattle country: Note the feed lot pens, hay bales and stock cars in the distance.

(Following page, bottom) Looking east, the ice dock and way car tracks are to the right. The large building at the left is the station and beyond is the three-story division office, where the division superintendent's car is parked on the siding. Beyond is the freight house. A fine Harvey House, the *Gran Quivera*, closed here in 1947. *(All, Robert A. Leilich)*

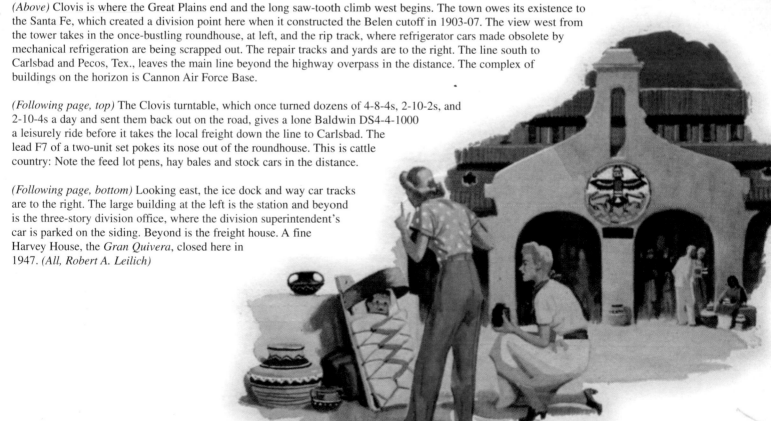

(Above) A couple railroaders lounge in the sun in front of the Clovis station on an unseasonably warm afternoon in February, 1966. Old Pelican has come in on #26 from Carlsbad, and the M.160 has just departed with #25, the southbound. The two motorcars trade off the run daily, an arrangement that will continue until 1967 when the train is dropped. Things are quiet for the moment, but a few freights will be along directly to keep the afternoon interesting. *(John P. Stroup)*

(Below) Motorcar M.160, the other half—some would say, the better half—of the team, awaits an 8:30 a.m. departure in front of the Carlsbad station, trailing round-end 3197. The 1932-built Brill car, which was dieselized in 1947 with a 535-hp turbocharged Sterling VDS-8, got the same beautification treatment at Albuquerque as sister M.190, including that classy Indian Head medallion on the side. The motorcar and its round-end will still take to the rails occasionally in the late 1990s, when the Age of Steam museum in Dallas sends the duo up the old Paris branch to Garland for various civic celebrations. *(J.J.Buckley)*

(Above) Eight units, evenly divided between SD24s and RSD7s, have 100 jumbo hoppers tied to their drawbars, out on one of the industrial spurs northeast of Carlsbad. The movement has evidently excited the interest of Santa Fe officials, several cars of which are parked at trackside. Because of sulfur and potash shipments, the Carlsbad area is one of Santa Fe's biggest money-makers. (Robert H. Leilich)

(Below) A "four-holer" Baldwin VO-1000 shuffles a way car at Clovis. Delivered during the war years, when Santa Fe took whatever switchers it could get and was grateful, the 20-year-old 2255 has given good service and is still valued for its impressive pulling power—60,000 pounds tractive effort. The road will install an EMD 567 engine in one of its Baldwins, the 2220, at Cleburne in December, 1970, resulting in a hybrid "Beep." But like so many hybrids, the result is ugly and not particularly successful, and 2255 and its 18 sisters will remain all-Baldwin until they are scrapped in 1971. (John P. Stroup)

(Above) While crews are busy taking off the Dallas cars and reshuffling the consist of the TEXAS CHIEF during its Gainesville stop, up at the head end the topic of conversation is the new U28CGs that have been assigned to the run, and whether they're better engines than the F7s they've replaced. On September 11, boiler-equipped 356 and its mates are only a few weeks old and still have red-painted pilots, soon to be repainted aluminum by Santa Fe. As for their performance, the engineer, leaning back so casually in the cab window, has had no trouble keeping #15 and its 22 cars on schedule on the 1,421-mile Chicago-Galveston run. The big U-boats will eventually lose their Warbonnets and migrate to freight service.

(Below) The mid-morning rush is about to hit Trinidad, Colo., Sept. 13, 1966. In short order, #23, THE GRAND CANYON and #17, THE SUPER CHIEF-EL CAPITAN will arrive from the east, and RSD7 609 and RSD5 2133 are waiting in the helper pocket to give one of the trains a shove over Raton Pass. The venerable Alcos, the only units ever assigned to Raton helper service on a regular basis, have been a familiar sight on the pass since the 1950s.

(Both, William Volkmer Collection)

(Right) Pulling out of Chillicothe, Ill., late on a September morning, #19, THE CHIEF, is running long, 20 cars including its familiar fulldome bar-lounge. The five-unit set of Fs will soon be working all out on the 1.1% up Edelstein Hill.

(Walter Peters,
Lou Schmitz Collection)

(Below) Coupled on behind the last coach of THE CHIEF on Oct. 7, 1966, is business car *Santa Fe*, assigned to the office of the president. That's him, right, Ernest K. Marsh, talking to L.M. Olson, general manager, Lines East.

(Roger E. Puta,
Melvern Finzer Collection)

(Below) Here's the reason for Ernest Marsh's presence in Chillicothe: In early October, Santa Fe has been conducting tests over the Illinois Division, taking priority consists from New York Central in Chicago and running them west as fast as five-unit sets of the new U28CGs can take them. East of Chillicothe, near Vernon, Ill., the 356 and its mates have 31 of New York Central's Flexi-vans and Santa Fe's dynamometer car running 84 mph. The train will hit 90 after ten of the cars are set out. A couple days later, another set of units will hit 86 mph with 29 standard TOFC flats. Although Flexi-vans create 31 percent less wind resistance, Santa Fe will conclude that standard TOFC operations offer greater flexibility and efficiency. Tests and joint marketing efforts by the two roads will continue into 1967, eventually leading to creation of SUPER-C, the world's fastest freight train. Telegraph pole at right offers a vantage point from which to observe 356's passage.

(Robert H. Leilich)

(Above) Nearing the end of its journey, a 51-car eastbound behind 327L-332B-318A will soon swing south across the Stevenson Expressway and enter Chicago's Corwith Yard. A second eastbound, with GP20s and a U25B, comes up alongside. Built for passenger service, the F7s are serving out their final years on freights in October, 1966. Modelers note: In A-units painted in the warbonnet scheme, only the panels behind the door and below the portholes are stainless steel. Other panels, doors and roof are aluminum-painted. B-units are all stainless steel except for roof and doors. (J.J.Buckley)

(Below) F3A 31L is still performing the service for which it was acquired, bringing Third #19 out of Dearborn. As THE CHIEF begins its westward trek, just two days before Independence Day, 1966, Santa Fe is still cautiously optimistic about passenger trains. The road is still the leader of the pack in the railroad passenger business, and will operate 14 million train miles this year, well ahead of Union Pacific's 8.4 and Burlington's 7.8 million. Two years ago, the Santa Fe even ordered 24 new hi-level cars for EL CAPITAN service. But ridership on THE CHIEF is slipping, and by this time next year will have fallen 10 percent, giving Chicago some second thoughts. (Lou Schmitz Collection)

(Above) Like an actor stepping into the spotlight, 343L glides momentarily into the afternoon sunlight at 21st Street Crossing, Chicago, with #17, THE SUPER CHIEF-EL CAPITAN in July, 1966. The 21st Street coach yards are at right. Santa Fe crosses Pennsylvania Railroad's line to Union Station here, while Erie Lackawanna, former Nickel Plate and Grand Trunk Western passenger trains turn east on Chicago & Western Indiana rails. (Matthew Herson, Jr.)

(Below) Perpetual Chicago switcher 2399 (see page 70) has probably rolled by this spot dozens of times a day in its 19-year-history, transferring strings of passengers cars between Dearborn Station and the 21st Street coach yards. Although classified as a road switcher, 2399 and its five sisters never get out on the road. The view from above emphasizes the extreme simplicity of the Alco design, first developed for U.S. Army service in World War II: radiator exhaust, engine hatches, engine exhaust, and, on the short hood, boiler exhaust. (Lou Schmitz Collection)

(Right) Four GP30s and a GP35—11,500 hp—rumble past East Tower at the Amarillo yard limits on Feb. 23, 1966 with an extra westbound. The tower's electromechanical interlocking plant controls crossings with Burlington's Fort Worth & Denver and the Rock Island, plus the junction with Santa Fe's line north to Las Animas, Colo. Amarillo is headquarters of the Plains Division. *(John P. Stroup)*

(Below) A set of PAs, a couple mail flats and lightweight cars can only mean one thing by spring, 1966: trains #1/2, THE SAN FRANCISCO CHIEF. At 10 a.m. March 12, there's just a handful of folks waiting on the platform at the Amarillo station as 52L-61A-56A-52C pull in with #1. Should any passenger from back east glance out the window, the handsome arches, stucco, and the tile roof on the 1910 station should leave no doubt that this is Santa Fe country. The schedule allows #1 20 minutes here.

(John P. Stroup)

Some 104 miles west, PAs 71L-62A-60A-78L accelerate after a 12:10 p.m. station stop at Clovis. Average speed from Amarillo to Clovis for the high-stepping Alcos: 56.5 mph.

(J.J. Buckley)

Having banged across Rock Island's Memphis-Tucumcari line, Extra 221C west is coming up on the Fort Worth & Denver crossing at Amarillo East Tower. The second two units—203B and 203C—were among the very first F7s acquired by Santa Fe, in 1949, and are running out their last miles. In July, 1970, the 203C will become the second unit to be rebuilt as a CF7, and, eventually, as the 2648, the oldest surviving CF7.

(Above) Mixed Train #37 for Las Animas, Colo., via Boise City, rattles through the crossovers at East Tower on March 12, 1966. The mixed, scheduled to leave Amarillo at 7:15 a.m., will be running on Plains Division rails as far as Boise City, 112.6 miles. The remaining 112.9 miles to Las Animas Junction, and the final 21-mile lap on the mainline to La Junta, are under the control of the Colorado Division. After the mixed clears the crossing, Rock Island's #22, with E7 636 in charge, will resume its long trek from Tucumcari. Santa Fe's mixed will long since have arrived at its destination when #22 pulls into Memphis, 20 hours from now.

(Left) The numbers on the signal inform us that we're at milepost 545.2, near Folsom, Tex., in automatic block signal territory east of Amarillo. Extra 914 west is making good time behind two SD24s and two RSD7s—Santa Fe likes to mix the big C-C units—and will arrive in the yards in ten minutes. (All, *John P. Stroup*)

Santa Fe Timeline

June 1967

(Below) We leap forward one year. What other railroad in June, 1967, can send out not just one or two, but a whole fleet of luxury streamliners, or can find enough business to run those streamliners in separate sections? For that matter, how many railroads' passenger trains still carry drumheads?

And yet this is the last hurrah for Santa Fe as generations of travelers have come to know it. In September, the U.S. Post Office Department will drop almost all of its mail contracts with the railroad, a $35 million loss of revenue, and a month later, president John S. Reed will announce an agonizing reappraisal of passenger operations. Both trains whose drumheads appear here side by side at La Junta, Colo., the SUPER CHIEF and EL CAPITAN, will carry on the tradition a couple years. So will the SAN FRANCISCO CHIEF, the TEXAS CHIEF and the SAN DIEGANS. But THE CHIEF and nine other trains will not survive, and Santa Fe will be a far different railroad.

As passenger service fades, however, there are exciting new things coming down the track: the world's fastest freight train, unit coal trains, and trains of containers moving at passenger train speeds and streetcar frequencies. Santa Fe will not disappear by any means—not for awhile, anyway—and the spectacle is not over. Join us for the show in the second volume as we follow **Santa Fe...all the way!**

SANTA FE ALL THE WAY

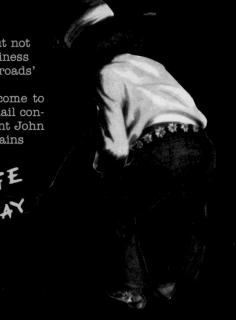

Bishop Brown,
May God bless you
ALWAYS!! Thank you
for everything.
Jose L. & Alicia Rodriguez

Well done
good and faithful
servant.
God bless you
Dn Matt & Patti Celeda

Dear Bishop,
Thank You very much
for being that gentle & caring
shepherd. We appreciated your
dedicated service in loving
support to the diaconate
community.
Gerhard & Cathy Stadel

With love, prayers & thanks—
many blessings — Mary Patronite
Thank You, Tony Patronite

May the Lord
bless you and
keep you.
Lovingly, Randy
Deacon Randy & Linda Marcon

Bishop Tod Brown
Thank you for sharing
your life and your
gifts with our
community. May God
continue to richly bless you
In His love,
Deacon Scott & Julie Ford

Bishop Brown,
Thank you, for
all you have given
to each & all of us
Deacon Jim and
Maria Cendeno

Bishop Brown
que el Sr lo bendiga
lo guarde de todo mal
y lo lleve a la vida
eterna
Diacono Jimmy y Marie
Mortimer

Dear Bishop Brown
Our family love you
so much. Thank you very
much and May God bless
you now and forever.
Dcn JOSEPH NGUYEN

Dear Brown,
Bishop Brown,
All the best from
one train fun to another!
And Bless you for everything
you have done for diocese +
the diaconate community and
your compassion a care for Cecilia.

God Bless you on your
retirement
Deacon Jerry L. Wilson

Dear Bishop Brown,
Wishing you a wonderful
and well deserved retirement
Bill & Sylvia Colbert

Dear Bishop Tod,
You have inspired and
encouraged me by your
love and devotion to our
Lord. Thank you and
may God bless you.
Deacon Richard and
Bev Dombeck

Dear Bishop
Thank you for your
spiritual leadership and all
that you have done for us.
God bless you with your
continuing journey.
Jim & Sally Arnold

Dear Bishop Brown,
May God Bless you
on your retirement
Deacon Phillip & Anna
Harijolinata

Dear Bishop Tod
Our Love Thoughts
and prayers go with
you. Thank you for
your leadership!
God Bless, Jim & Candi
Merle

Bishop Tod
Happy Travels & Joy
To You In The Years
To Come!
Deacon Charlie &
Linda Boyer

Bishop Brown,
Happy Retirement, BUT
You are always our bishop
and pray for all of us!
Hope to see you around
for the years to come.
Deacon Peter Chung & Clare

Thanks for "training"
our group - your flock!
Dear Bishop Brown
sentiro molto la
vostra presenza
con effetto
Rose Thompson